Cambridge Elements ≣

Elements in Experimental Political Science
edited by
James N. Druckman
Northwestern University

SHOULD YOU STAY AWAY FROM STRANGERS?

Experiments on the Political Consequences of Intergroup Contact

Ethan Busby
Brigham Young University

CAMBRIDGE
UNIVERSITY PRESS

University Printing House, Cambridge CB2 8BS, United Kingdom

One Liberty Plaza, 20th Floor, New York, NY 10006, USA

477 Williamstown Road, Port Melbourne, VIC 3207, Australia

314–321, 3rd Floor, Plot 3, Splendor Forum, Jasola District Centre, New Delhi – 110025, India

79 Anson Road, #06–04/06, Singapore 079906

Cambridge University Press is part of the University of Cambridge.

It furthers the University's mission by disseminating knowledge in the pursuit of education, learning, and research at the highest international levels of excellence.

www.cambridge.org
Information on this title: www.cambridge.org/9781108958448
DOI: 10.1017/9781108957885

First published 2021

A catalogue record for this publication is available from the British Library.

ISBN 978-1-108-95844-8 Paperback
ISSN 2633-3368 (online)
ISSN 2633-335X (print)

Should You Stay Away from Strangers?

Experiments on the Political Consequences of Intergroup Contact

Elements in Experimental Political Science

DOI: 10.1017/9781108957885
First published online: February 2021

Ethan Busby
Brigham Young University
Author for correspondence: Ethan Busby, ethan.busby@byu.edu

Abstract: Harmonious relationships between groups are critical for democracy, and intergroup contact presents an appealing way to encourage this harmony. However, what kinds of contact work best? Ethan Busby reviews existing studies of contact, proposes a framework for studying the political consequences of contact, and discusses four experiments following these recommendations. These studies focus on equal-status contact and rely on different samples and contexts. Busby finds that equal status does not promote more political support for racial and ethnic outgroups and can reduce outgroup support. The Element is concluded by discussing the implications of these findings for the study of contact generally.

Keywords: intergroup contact, experiments, political psychology, race, status

ISBNs: 9781108958448 (PB), 9781108957885 (OC)
ISSNs: 2633-3368 (online), 2633-335X (print)

Contents

1 Introduction

Social groups are a critical part of political life. However, group attachments and thinking can lead to conflict, prejudice, and intolerance. In response to this reality, many political theorists propose that harmonious relationships between groups provide democracies with important benefits and are *requirements* for democratic government (Barber 1984; Dahl 1989; Taylor 1994). From this point of view, attitudes toward outgroups – groups to which one does not belong – are especially important, as many people spontaneously provide tolerance, inclusivity, and recognition to members of their own groups (e.g., Balliet, Wu, and De Dreu 2014; Greenwald and Pettigrew 2014). The challenge for democratic societies, then, lies in promoting tolerance, inclusivity, and support toward outgroups.

In this Element, I consider this challenge directly, examining one prominent avenue for improving support for other groups: intergroup contact. In the sections that follow, I summarize contact research, explore the application of this work to political science, and discuss the limitations of those studies. I then present an outline of this Element, which lays out a framework for studying contact through experimental methods. Using this framework as a guide, I describe a set of four experiments that explore the democratic consequences of different kinds of interracial and interethnic contact. These studies consider multiple facets of contact: the difficulty of communicating across groups, the decision to opt in or out of contact, the durability of contact's effects, and more. The results of these experiments reveal important insights into the political role of intergroup contact; specifically, they suggest that common forms of intergroup interactions can promote more positive impressions of outgroup individuals. However, those impressions and contact experiences do not translate into political support for outgroups. In fact, such encounters can, under some conditions, *undermine* support for other groups.

1.1 The Promise of Intergroup Contact?

Social scientists have devoted a great deal of effort to understanding individuals' attitudes and behaviors toward social groups. By social groups, I mean subsets of individuals, the boundaries of which are recognized by those who do and do not belong to that group (Tajfel 1982). These include religious groups (Protestants, Jews, Muslims, Hindus, etc.), political groups (Democrats, Republicans, Independents, etc.), racial and ethnic groups (African Americans, Latinxs[1], Whites, etc.), and more.

---

[1] I use the terms Latinx and Latinxs, instead of the more common Latino or Latina, to avoid gendered language when speaking about individuals.

One of the more troubling conclusions of this work is the persistent finding that people strongly prefer their own groups and seem all too willing to lash out against other groups. In a general sense, these patterns can lead to prejudice, intolerance, and distrust (e.g., Greenwald and Pettigrew 2014; Fiske 2015; Vermue, Seger, and Sanfey 2018). In the realm of politics, many majority group members defensively react against social and demographic change with increased support for anti-minority beliefs and political ideologies (e.g., Craig and Richeson 2014b; Abrajano and Hajnal 2015). Ethnocentrism, or a strong preference for one's own groups over others, shapes reactions to political candidates, support for war, and more (Kinder and Kam 2009; Kam and Kinder 2012). Media messages amplify these tendencies and prime group-based ideas (Mendelberg 2001; Hopkins 2010; Klar 2013). This tendency to think in groups and take sides seems to be increasing in the political world (Iyengar, Sood, and Lelkes 2012; Mason 2018; Jardina 2019), posing major challenges to democratic societies.

Given these troubling findings, social scientists have vigorously explored ways to promote harmony, understanding, and tolerance between groups. One prominent body of research considers how interactions between groups (inter-group contact) can promote positive attitudes toward, and tolerance for, those groups. Drawing on a foundation of ideas from the mid-twentieth century (e.g., Allport 1954; Blalock 1967), contact theory suggests that when experiences between group members occur under certain circumstances, these encounters promote more understanding, tolerance, and support for social outgroups. Most famously, Allport (1954) suggested four key conditions that promote under-standing between groups: equal status, collaboration, common goals, and authority approval. Others have added additional conditions, such as friendship potential (Pettigrew 1998) and group salience (Voci and Hewstone 2003), but the original four continue to hold a special place in contact theory.

A large body of empirical research concludes that intergroup experiences improve group harmony. For example, diverse classroom settings correspond with reductions in group-based prejudice (Patchen 1982; Stringer et al. 2009), interracial roommate arrangements reduce prejudice and interracial anxieties (Shook and Fazio 2008), workplace contact and intergroup friendships reduce anti-foreigner sentiments (Sønderskov and Thomsen 2015; Tropp et al. 2018), and contact with outgroups can increase support for political policies in favor of those groups (Barth and Parry 2009; Finseraas and Kotsadam 2017). As such, intergroup contact seems to offer a promising path to the tolerance, support, and inclusivity advocated for by democratic theorists.

Underneath these positive findings, however, a string of criticisms has devel-oped into a robust counter-literature. These critiques include concerns about the contact experiences researchers usually study (Dixon, Durrheim, and Tredoux 2005; MacInnis and Page-Gould 2015), gaps in understanding what predicts negative reactions to contact (Pettigrew 2008; Paolini, Harwood, and Rubin 2010; Barlow et al. 2012), and summaries of this literature that point out severe methodological and inferential limitations in many existing studies (Paluck, Green, and Green 2018).

Uncertainty about the effects of contact increases further when political scientists attempt to connect the attitudes and behaviors explored by psychologists to the types of political support and tolerance that are critical to democratic societies. Researchers who make too quick a leap from the attitude- and prejudice-focused variables considered in psychology to more political or collective concepts may unintentionally lead themselves astray. By and large, contact research has emphasized reducing prejudice and anti-outgroup attitudes, and it is here that contact research has the most consistent results (Pettigrew and Tropp 2011). However, individual-level prejudice and outgroup attitudes may or may not operate similar to more political concepts, like support for affirmative action policies or tolerance for specific kinds of political demonstrations. For example, individuals often maintain a gap between their general attitudes and their willingness to support concrete policies or political actions related to those attitudes; this is the so-called principle-implementation or principle-policy gap that has been robustly documented with regards to racial attitudes and racial policies (Jackman 1978; 1996; Rabinowitz et al. 2009; Tuch and Hughes 2011). This gap seems to persist in the face of intergroup contact: empirical studies considering political attitudes have a mixed track record of extending the effects of contact to specific political attitudes, sometimes finding that contact increases political support for outgroups, has no effect, or reduces support for collective action in support of outgroups (e.g., Jackman and Crane 1986; Barth and Parry 2009; Cakal et al. 2011; Enos 2014). Similarly, contact studies that focus on support for concrete political and social action find that some forms of contact may improve attitudes while simultaneously undermining support for actions and movements addressing group-based inequities (Saguy et al. 2009; Dixon et al. 2010; Reimer et al. 2017; Bagci and Turnuklu 2019).

As such, the overall picture from contact research remains unclear. While a popular notion among academics and the public, the proposition that contact improves group relationships has, at best, only mixed empirical support. In the end, social scientists and policymakers still wrestle with the same question proposed by Allport and the original versions of contact theory: Under what conditions does contact generate more or less political support for outgroups?

1.2 Moving Forward

In response to this lingering question, this Element proposes a framework for studying the political consequences of intergroup contact through experiments. As discussed in Section 2, carefully designed experiments provide an avenue for considering what forms of intergroup contact promote and discourage increased political support for social outgroups. This framework requires researchers to intentionally create specific forms of intergroup contact, integrate multiple relevant social science theories, consider a range of attitudes and behaviors, and intentionally design experiments to boost external validity. Contributing to the large and mixed literature on contact requires this type of systematic and careful research; otherwise, additional studies are unlikely to clarify the consequences of intergroup experiences. In the rest of the Element, I apply this framework by reporting on four experiments that: (1) focus on short interactions with strangers, varying the difficulty of communicating; (2) compare contact and group threat theory; (3) consider political, interpersonal, and behavioral outcomes; and (4) rely on different samples and varying treatments to improve the generalizability of the experiments.

Section 3 demonstrates this framework in an initial study of interracial contact. In this laboratory experiment, respondents interacted with trained outgroup members who varied their nonverbal behavior (eye contact, pauses, body language, etc.) in ways that made them easier or harder to understand and correspond with Allport's condition of equal status. The results of this experiment indicate that interracial contact that is structured to improve communications between groups does not improve political support and tolerance for outgroups. Instead, it can undermine, rather than bolster, White Americans' political support for racial outgroups. In this setting, easy-to-understand interracial contact fails to produce an increase in political support for racial outgroups the way contact theory would predict.

Section 4 evaluates the temporal, contextual, and sample-based limitations of Section 3 through three additional experiments. These three experiments build on the earlier study by considering the choice to engage in contact, the specific group division involved in contact, and differences in the medium through which contact occurs. These studies both support the findings of the first experiment and indicate the limitations of applying those conclusions in an overly broad way. In the end, the full set of experiments provides much broader insight into the role of intergroup contact in democratic societies. Section 5 summarizes the results of all four experiments and brings them into conversation with the framework proposed in Section 2.

The approach I advocate for in this Element allows researchers interested in contact to contribute to ongoing academic, political, and social debates about how to improve group relationships and to do so in a way that relies on solid causal inferences and robust research designs. As social diversity increases in established democracies and changes in the technological environment make more and more types of social experiences possible, careful studies of intergroup contact are needed now more than ever.

2 A Framework for Studying Intergroup Contact

To date, contact theory has enjoyed a long, productive tradition in the social sciences. Reviews of this body of research often conclude that contact nearly always results in a reduction of prejudice and increase in pro-outgroup attitudes (e.g., Pettigrew and Tropp 2011). However, this consensus is far less universal than it seems at first glance. Here, I briefly review contact research and conclude that the main question posed by the original proponents of contact theory – when contact improves and worsens social divisions – remains unanswered. I then propose a framework relying on specific kinds of experiments to productively answer this question about the role of groups and group divisions in democratic politics.

2.1 Proponents of Contacts

As summarized in the previous section, social science research on contact is extensive and largely falls into two camps: those who conclude that contact has a positive effect on intergroup attitudes and those who are more skeptical. An exhaustive review of research on contact is outside of the scope of this Element and is better accomplished with meta-analyses than narrative reviews of the literature. However, the following section describes the main conclusions and limitations of this research as a backdrop for the ideas and experiments that follow.

Contact theory proposes that interactions between members of different groups improve attitudes toward outgroups, reduce prejudice, and address the problems often created by group divisions. The original formulations of this theory suggested that contact would only provide these benefits when specific conditions were met (Allport 1954; Pettigrew 1998). Most prominent among these are four original criteria suggested by Allport that continue to permeate contact research: collaboration, common goals, authority approval, and equal status. Collaboration suggests that people in the contact experience actively work together, as opposed to ignoring one another or completing tasks isolated from one another. Common goals indicates that participants' objectives align closely, which prevents competition between social groups in the contact experience. Authority approval involves the explicit endorsement of a contact scenario by influential figures of some kind (religious leaders, government officials, military officers, etc.). Finally, equal status focuses on the position of individuals within the contact experience – are participants placed on equal footing within the interaction and positioned as social equals? This kind of status can be conveyed in different ways, ranging from membership in different socioeconomic groups to the amount of competence and confidence individuals convey (Riordan 1978; Riordan and Ruggiero 1980).

Allport's conditions connect to key ideas about power and politics, making these conditions relevant for political scientists as well as psychologists. For example, some link authority approval to the messages sent by prominent Democrats and Republicans about racial and ethnic groups (Pearson-Merkowitz, Filindra, and Dyck 2015). Even more so, equal status has special relevance to political science and theories of democracy. Deliberative theories of democracy often require equality and mutual respect between participants in deliberation (Thompson 2008; Mansbridge et al. 2012). Without this equal status, deliberation does not serve to improve the quality of democracy or operate as intended (S. Chambers 2003, 322). Other versions of democratic theory list mutual tolerance, recognition, and equality between citizens as criteria that define democratic societies (Dahl 1989; Taylor 1994; Mansbridge et al. 2010) – these standards are difficult, if not impossible, to meet without equal status. The connections further emphasize the importance of contact research and discussions of the four original conditions to scholars of politics and democracy.

Many empirical studies are supportive of contact theory, providing evidence that intergroup experiences could benefit individuals, groups, and society. This evidence comes from a variety of settings, including in schools (Robinson and Preston 1976; Cohen and Lotan 1995), neighborhoods (Deutsch and Collins 1951; Wilner, Walkley, and Cook 1955), the military (e.g., Moskos and Butler 1996), and sports teams (Brown et al. 2003). A prominent review of contact research has found strong evidence in line with these individual articles, concluding that contact reduces prejudice toward specific outgroup members, the group an individual is associated with, and even unrelated groups. Relying on an extensive meta-analysis of more than 500 empirical studies, this research finds that the benefits of contact seem robust to publication bias, geographical location, the immediate setting of contact, the age of the individuals in the contact encounter, general quality of the research, and different types of group divisions like race, age, gender, sexual orientation, and more (Pettigrew and Tropp 2011). Ultimately, the authors conclude that their findings "provide compelling evidence that intergroup contact is universally useful in reducing prejudice across a great range of intergroup situations" (Pettigrew and Tropp 2011, 61). Because of its scope and depth, this meta-analysis forms the bedrock of current contact research – as an illustration, publications from this analysis have been cited more than 10,000 times. And while the meta-analysis is not the final word on contact – newer studies explore other elements of contact such as the role of contact in computer mediated settings (e.g., Alvídrez et al. 2015) or placing intergroup contact within larger social, political, and temporal contexts (such as Paolini et al. 2014; Enos and Celaya 2018) – most make some kind of connection to this thorough summary of contact theory.

2.2 Contact's Critics

Despite this large body of research, a consistent group of researchers remains skeptical about the positive potential of contact. These critiques center on two major points: what counts as contact and the original conditions of contact.[2]

The first of these issues is how to decide which social experiences count as contact. In the original formulation of contact theory, Allport proposed that not all kinds of intergroup interactions were equivalent; his discussion covered at least four different kinds of experiences, including causal interactions, acquaintances, neighborhoods, and workplaces (Allport 1954, 262). Social experiences with outgroups can differ both in the specific relationship people have with the outgroup member and the characteristics of the encounter itself. These relationships can range in intimacy from immediate family members to complete strangers. The characteristics of contact can differ in both location – e.g., work, home, the bowling alley, etc. – and duration – e.g., a few minutes, weeks, or years. For example, intergroup contact can occur with a coworker over the course of a months-long collaboration, or someone could experience contact with a stranger as they are visiting a grocery store. Should academics and policymakers treat all of these different experiences the same way?

With few exceptions, contact research sidesteps these questions even though the implications of contact with these different features may vary greatly. Most research simply chooses one kind of social experience to study without much consideration or explanation; for example, some focus on in-depth interactions with strangers (e.g., Trawalter and Richeson 2008), others on the importance of close outgroup friendships (Turner et al. 2007; Newman 2014), and still others on the mere physical presence of outgroup members (e.g., Enos 2014; Sands

---

[2] There are other important, less explored criticisms of contact research, such as that contact may simultaneously reduce prejudice among advantaged groups while undermining support for social change among disadvantaged groups (Saguy et al. 2009; Dixon et al. 2010; Glasford and Calcagno 2012).

2017). The rare studies that have directly compared various kinds of intergroup interactions often find that both the amount and intimacy of contact influence how much it reduces prejudicial attitudes (Jackman and Crane 1986; Stringer et al. 2009; Ellison, Shin, and Leal 2011); attempts to harmonize these different choices indicate that what researchers conclude from their study of contact depends on what kinds of social experiences they examine (MacInnis and Page-Gould 2015). At a more basic level, most studies of contact are not clear enough on what kind of contact they consider and why they make those choices; a recent attempt to summarize current experimental research on contact ultimately concludes that researchers report too little detail about the version of contact they consider for others to replicate or even categorize these studies (Paluck, Green, and Green 2018).

A second area of concern about contact research is the status of Allport's original four conditions. As mentioned already, Allport and some of the research that followed him considered these conditions to be crucial to reducing prejudice and group-based bias through contact. Some take issue with these conditions from a theoretical perspective. One critique centers on how different perspectives in the social sciences would predict different things about authority approval, common goals, cooperation, and equal status. From the view of racial threat theory, for example, prejudice stems from a feeling of superiority and privilege among advantaged groups and a fear that subordinate groups will attempt to take away those privileges. Efforts to intrude on the status of majority groups therefore arouse suspicion and antipathy (Blumer 1958, 5). Numerous empirical studies support this perspective, concluding that when people perceive threats to their social position from outgroups, they display more prejudice and political opposition to those groups (e.g., Key 1949; Quillian 1995; Bobo and Hutchings 1996; Norton and Sommers 2011; Enos 2016; Mutz 2018). The conditions proposed by Allport could be perceived as attempts to undermine the position of one's own group. For example, members of majority groups may feel threatened by equal-status contact experiences, as these encounters undermine both their view of the group-based hierarchy and threaten privileges they enjoy. Consequently, this would translate to increased prejudice and a lack of political support for these groups.

Empirically, support for the conditions is also more mixed than it seems on the surface. On one level, some specific studies find that Allport's conditions magnify the benefits of intergroup contact (e.g., Riordan and Ruggiero 1980; Gaertner et al. 1990; Cohen and Lotan 1995; Pearson-Merkowitz, Filindra, and Dyck 2015). However, attempts to summarize this literature have been far less conclusive. The major meta-analytic summary of contact research concludes that the four basic conditions are not necessary to generate pro-outgroup reactions (Pettigrew and Tropp 2011). Specifically reviewing studies that emphasized one or more of the conditions, the authors find that intergroup contact typically results in a moderate reduction in anti-outgroup attitudes even when the key conditions proposed by contact theory are absent. The authors ultimately state that "Allport's conditions are not essential for intergroup contact to achieve positive outcomes ... [and] should not be regarded as necessary" (Pettigrew and Tropp 2006, 766; see also 2011, 67–68). This conclusion contrasts sharply with Allport's ideas, as he warned that many forms of intergroup experiences would exacerbate, rather than address, group differences (Allport 1954, 263). An updated, more focused meta-analysis raises additional concerns on this point, finding that no recent experimental studies of contact explicitly considered and randomized any of Allport's conditions. The results of the meta-analysis lead the authors to conclude that even when researchers document that contact reduces prejudice, "we learn little about what specific aspects of the contact are reducing participants' prejudice" (Paluck, Green, and Green 2018, 25).

In brief, the following points emerge as major conclusions from research on the democratic benefits of intergroup contact:

- *Allport proposed that contact could, under specific conditions, reduce prejudice and resolve conflicts between groups. This proposition created an expansive body of research.*
- *Despite this, two points remain unclear: what experiences count as intergroup contact and what role Allport's conditions play.*
- *As a result, the basic question posed by Allport – when contact can resolve problems between groups – remains unanswered.*

2.3 A Productive, Experimental Framework

In response to these lingering uncertainties, I propose the following framework for productively studying the political consequences of intergroup contact through randomized experiments. This perspective recommends that contact experiments include four components: (1) controlled, researcher-created social experiences; (2) the integration of other competing social science theories like those on group threat theory, stereotypes, and conversational norms; (3) measuring a range of attitudes and behaviors; and (4) intentional design choices to boost generalizability. I begin with a discussion of the benefits of the experimental method in this area and then take up each part of the proposed framework.

2.3.1 The Experimental Method

A review of political science research about intergroup contact reveals that experiments in this area are rare; instead, many studies rely on observational data paired with details about the geographic and social environments in which individuals reside (e.g., Oliver and Mendelberg 2000; Barth, Overby, and Huffmon 2009). While there are some creative and important exceptions (e.g., Enos 2014; Sands 2017), by and large, political scientists rely on observational and survey data to understand how interactions with social others influence political attitudes and behaviors. To a lesser extent, the same is true of psychology research on contact; in the most extensive meta-analysis, for example, only 5 percent of contact studies used experimental designs (Pettigrew and Tropp 2006, 759).

There are many advantages to these nonexperimental approaches. These kinds of data allow for explorations of real-world trends and representative slices of different communities. Further, they can consider comparisons across time, showing how patterns of intergroup experiences shift with contemporary political and social events (such as Sigelman et al. 1996; Eller and Abrams 2004).

However, nonexperimental approaches face key limitations. First and foremost, these studies may suffer from selection bias. Individuals can self-select into different forms of contact based on their preexisting views about social groups. If researchers do not randomly assign contact, then, whatever motivates this self-selection may confound any observed relationship between contact and group-based attitudes. Observational research on contact often wrestles with this possibility, considering if contact reduces prejudice, if prejudice reduces contact, or both (Binder et al. 2009).

Observational approaches also leave open precisely what counts as contact. Many such studies measure contact using self-reports of interaction with groups or overall geographic diversity. But such diversity does not ensure intergroup contact of any particular kind, and self-reports fail to capture differences in what people count as friendships, contacts, etc. This raises questions about what exactly intergroup contact entails, how comparable contact is across studies, and if "effects" from contact are really the product of something else (institutional rules, historical experiences, etc.). For example, is it fair to equate someone who lives in a racially diverse area with someone with a racially diverse extended family? Does everyone mean the same thing when they say they come into "contact" with minority groups? These questions are particularly important given some of the differences described earlier in studies that emphasize different kinds of intergroup contact.

Experimental methods can respond to both limitations. In an experimental design, individuals can be directly assigned to have different experiences, independent of their preexisting attitudes, environments, or characteristics. This kind of design therefore allows researchers to isolate the effects of a particular interaction. Additionally, experiments allow researchers to create specific kinds of interactions intentionally (like contact that does and does not meet Allport's conditions), considering specific aspects of contact while holding everything else constant. An added benefit of this approach is that these designs can say with certainty what a specific version of contact entails, as the intergroup experiences are structured in specific, knowable ways.

Using experiments, however, does not resolve all of the challenges in studying contact. Selecting an experimental method requires researchers to make a series of specific choices that are often left undiscussed, undocumented, and unjustified. These types of decisions can cause problems in replicability and comparisons between different designs (Paluck, Green, and Green 2018). To help avoid these problems, I lay out four elements of contact experiments that can promote a clearer theoretical understanding of the role of contact and make contact research more useful for academics, policymakers, and the public.

2.3.2 Controlled, Researcher-Created Social Experiences

One of the first decisions a contact researcher faces is what kind of contact to study. An experimental paradigm cannot escape this issue – researchers designing the experiment must decide what kind of contact to create. The options are nearly limitless, ranging from the mere presence of outgroup individuals (such as Enos 2014) to lengthy, more structured persuasive appeals (e.g., Broockman and Kalla 2016). Should experimental subjects be allowed to interact with one another in a relatively free-flowing and unsupervised way? Or should some of the participants be a scripted, carefully planned part of the study itself?

Here I advocate for the use of trained confederates – individuals who are a planned, designed part of the study unbeknownst to the subjects. In this approach, a contact experience involves one naive subject and one trained individual who acts and speaks in predetermined ways. This has the disadvantage of requiring a larger sample size, since each interaction involves only one respondent instead of two or more. In addition, it means researchers must recruit, train, and supervise these confederates, often with few guidelines about how to do so. Consequently, many studies using these types of designs are executed with limited sample sizes as a result of time and resource constraints (e.g., Nisbett and Cohen 1996; Trawalter and Richeson 2008; cf., Sands 2017).

However, trained confederates offer the critical benefit of clear, precise control over the behavior of the outgroup member in the contact experience. This is crucial given the confusion between different studies about what contact entails. Control over the outgroup member means that experimenters directly manipulate elements of the intergroup contact intentionally. This type of experiment can therefore directly answer the central question of contact research: What factors promote positive and negative reactions to intergroup contact? For example, confederates can speak and behave in ways that correspond to Allport's (1954) conditions or other basic elements of interpersonal interactions.

This approach has other benefits. It is often important for the outgroup member to unambiguously be a member of the intended outgroup; otherwise, the group dynamics the researcher intended to study may be absent (Pettigrew and Tropp 2011). By controlling outgroup member behavior and appearance, trained confederates allow the researcher to make group divisions salient and unambiguous. Confederates can use racially stereotypical names, say they are from racialized areas, wear clothing marking group status, etc. This makes the corresponding group division more accessible in the subjects' minds, which is another important element of intergroup experiences (see Voci and Hewstone 2003; Paolini, Harwood, and Rubin 2010). An additional benefit of this approach is that it clarifies precisely what type of experience contact involves. This type of controlled form of contact forces researchers to make choices about the setting where contact occurs, the length of contact, what type of larger social experience the experimental version is intended to mimic, etc. Insofar as scholars are clear about these decisions, controlled contact through confederates can improve comparability and replicability between contact studies.

One critique of this approach is that it may create misleading estimates of contact's effects because contact in these kinds of experiments are, at some level, involuntary. Some suggest that involuntary contact is more likely to lead to negative reactions than voluntary experiences (Pettigrew and Tropp 2011). However, researchers can address these concerns by evaluating these possibilities in their experimental designs and interpretation. The experiments that follow illustrate one way to do just that.

Another concern about such experimental control of contact is that it undermines the ability of the experiment to speak to real-world forms of contact. By making one person in the contact experience a controlled, scripted part of the experiment, the contact experience may not unfold as naturally as it would if both individuals were experiencing a genuine kind of contact. This concern is similar to many critiques of experiments that note the way a stimuli or treatment in an experiment does not accurately match the concept of interest in the real world; to use methodological language, contact experiments using confederates may be lacking in "mundane realism" and corresponding external validity.

Researcher-controlled forms of contact can still offer significant benefits in spite of this concern. Experimental realism, or how seriously subjects engage with the experiment and find it to be believable, is more important to the central goals and causal inferences of experiments than mundane realism (Berkowitz and Donnerstein 1982; McDermott 2002; Druckman and Kam 2011). Contact experiments can incorporate high amounts of experimental realism when scripts are designed well, confederates are extensively trained and practiced, and the experiment is constructed so that subjects are unaware of the way the confederate is giving scripted responses. The need for clearer causal inferences in contact research further motivates an emphasis on experimental rather than mundane realism. Researchers can also acknowledge the ways their experiments have reduced amounts of mundane realism and make explicit design choices to bolster that form of generalizability, a topic discussed later in this Element. The examples that follow in this Element make explicit choices to create contact experiences that most accurately mimic the type of intergroup experiences individuals have in the real world and, by so doing, maximize experimental and mundane realism as much as possible.

Even if studies of contact do not create intergroup experiences as I recommend, it is critical that researchers indicate what form of contact they are considering, how they create that kind of contact, and the reasons behind these decisions. Detailed appendices containing scripts, descriptions of treatment specifics, photos of confederates, and more are key to evaluating and replicating studies of intergroup contact. These materials have improved as discussions of transparency and replication have increased, but it can still be challenging to design experiments based on the procedures and materials used by others.

- *Element 1: Directly create contact in experiments and be transparent about these choices.*

2.3.3 Integration of Other Competing Social Science Theories

The second part of the proposed framework is to incorporate various theoretical approaches when studying contact. Social science research on groups is extensive, reaching into psychology, sociology, political science, economics, and beyond. Any single study need not be all-inclusive, but failing to engage various theoretical ideas limits researchers' inferences and conclusions.

This suggestion is not new. In one meta-analysis, for example, the authors consider how theories on intergroup threat and contact can be connected into a combined set of more complete expectations (Pettigrew and Tropp 2011, 196). This allows those authors to respond to some of their more prominent critics and propose a more developed theoretical model about intergroup contact. By integrating perspectives on group-based threat, these authors begin to provide theoretical expectations for the results of both positive and negative forms of contact. While more still needs to be done in this vein, this bridging between theories allows this meta-analysis to expand its scope and contribution to different schools of thought in psychology.

The combination of intergroup threat and contact research is a natural place to combine different theories because the two approaches have different perspectives on contact and Allport's original conditions. As discussed previously, group threat approaches conclude that contact, even and especially under Allport's conditions, can reinforce group differences, highlight threats to an ingroup's status and benefits, and ultimately undermine political support for outgroups. Considering the role of group threat, then, allows researchers to consider and evaluate these predictions alongside the ideas of contact research.

Additional theories could also be combined with contact theory. For example, theories about conversational norms can provide insight into the expectations people bring into intergroup experiences (Grice 1975). These theories about conversational expectations provide concrete predictions about the centrality of *how* people speak in contact settings instead of just *what* is said (a point to which I return later). Research on stereotypes and how to interrupt the use of stereotypes could also be linked to contact (Devine 1989; Fiske et al. 2002; Fiske 2015), suggesting different reactions to outgroups with different preexisting stereotypes and when specific outgroup individuals do or do not conform to more general stereotypes of their groups. Political scientists can further bolster contact theory by bringing in discussions about the nature of power, larger group-based hierarchies, and the implications of institutional elements of society (e.g., Bachrach and Baratz 1962; Lukes 1974; King and Smith 2011). This kind of theory building helps explore and expand discussions of the processes involved in intergroup contact, another gap in contact literature (Paluck, Green, and Green 2018).

- *Element 2: Integrate multiple theoretical perspectives about the role of contact.*

2.3.4 Consideration of a Range of Attitudes and Behaviors

As noted earlier, one area of concern in contact research is how much contact influences behaviors and attitudes beyond prejudice. This is especially important in the realm of political science, which explores contact's potential to generate attitudes and behaviors that benefit democratic societies. Political scientists have noted that individuals frequently maintain a gap between their general sentiments toward social groups and their concrete policy views and behaviors (Jackman 1978; 1996; Rabinowitz et al. 2009; Tuch and Hughes 2011). As such, experiments on intergroup contact can be improved by including broader measures of individuals' attitudes and evaluating the principle-policy gap in response to contact. Focusing on a larger set of outcomes would also help document the boundaries of contact's effects and explain the mixed findings from extending the effects of contact to specific political attitudes.

This recommendation is especially important for political scientists. Typically, political scientists focus on the political, democratic, and power-based consequences of prejudice and group divisions (e.g., Key 1949; Kinder and Sears 1981; Huddy and Feldman 2009; Kinder and Kam 2009; Blinder, Ford, and Ivarsflaten 2013). This suggests that studies considering the political consequences of contact require broader measures than those used by most psychological studies.

In practice, this means researchers should include measures of individuals' political views, political tolerance, concrete interpersonal choices, and impressions of the outgroup individual. Doing so creates a more complete picture of the larger democratic importance of contact experiences. It also more directly connects contact research to interventions and concrete policy outcomes. As this usually means adding additional survey questions, the benefits outweigh the costs of focusing only on prejudice reduction.

- *Element 3: Measure a broad range of attitudes and behaviors in response to contact.*

2.3.5 Intentional Choices to Evaluate Generalizability

Finally, those studying contact with experiments should intentionally design their studies with generalizability in mind. Experiments are often criticized for applying only to narrow populations and very specific circumstances (see Sears 1986; Druckman and Kam 2011); in some ways, this is the root issue behind many concerns about replicability in social science research (e.g., Open Science Collaboration 2015). Seriously considering how to design these experiments to improve external validity, then, will improve experimental designs on any topic.

This is especially true of intergroup contact. Research in this area is far past the basic demonstration that contact can influence attitudes and behavior and now struggles with specifying conditions in which contact produces different results. Details like the sample, context, and durability provide a more complete picture of contact and address some of the discrepancies between findings in existing studies.

Taking generalizability seriously involves planning follow-up experiments to evaluate the same form of contact in other settings, specifically considering different populations of subjects, using multi-wave studies to evaluate decay, and conducting experiments in a cumulative way. This requires a longer-term perspective but offers the benefit of a clearer understanding of contact, more robust causal inferences, and a direct consideration of one of the main limits of experiments as a method.

• *Element 4: Design contact experiments with generalizability in mind.*

2.4 Applications to Follow

For the rest of this Element, I implement this proposed framework in a set of experiments. In Section 3, I discuss an experimental study of interracial contact that varies the difficulty of understanding an outgroup member. Section 4 further implements this framework through three additional in-person and online survey experiments. All of these experiments apply the parts of the framework discussed here and have three other common elements: (1) an emphasis on brief interactions with strangers, (2) the group division of race and ethnicity, and (3) manipulation of the difficulty of understanding the outgroup member. These common components allow the studies to build on each other and apply the proposed recommendations.

2.4.1 The Encounter

Given the confusion about what counts as contact, I focus on one important type of intergroup contact: brief interactions with outgroup strangers. In other words, short conversations between people without an existing social relationship. Although common, this social experience remains understudied. In everyday life, such experiences include conversations with fellow commuters, interactions with store clerks or cashiers, and encounters with those asking for money or political support. Many people have these types of encounters regularly, and survey data on how Americans spend their time indicates that in any given day, 13 percent of American adults have one-on-one experiences with strangers.[3] Over months or years, almost everyone has countless such experiences.

---

[3] More information on the survey and data is publicly available online (www.bls.gov/tus/#data). The data range from 2003 to 2016, although results are similar using only 2016.

Interactions with strangers are also a primary point where individuals interact with people from other social groups. People are generally geographically surrounded by members of ingroups rather than outgroups (Bishoff and Reardon 2014; Motyl et al. 2014; Rugh and Massey 2014), and social networks are typically quite homogeneous (DiPrete et al. 2011). This is true for various kinds of group divisions, including race, political views, and economic status. In such environments, strangers are a key point of contact with outgroups since they are absent from more established social ties; documenting various forms of interracial experiences, for example, finds that interracial contact "consists primarily of brief, superficial encounters" (Sigelman et al. 1996, 1306). Even if one does encounter outgroups among neighbors or friends, interactions with strangers likely still matter due to their frequency and the increased proportion of outgroup members in these settings.

Despite their frequency, very little existing research considers these types of social encounters. Psychological work that creates contact in lab settings frequently directly brings up group differences (e.g., race), differentiating it from the conversations most people are likely to have with strangers (e.g., Trawalter and Richeson 2008). Some political psychology studies create more realistic encounters with strangers but in scenarios that do not require the strangers to interact (Enos 2014; Sands 2017). Here I take a difference approach, looking to understand the kinds of brief encounters with strangers most people have most of the time. Modeling the experiences that occur in normal life simultaneously addresses some criticisms of contact research (Dixon, Durrheim, and Tredoux 2005) and buttresses the generalizability of the empirical work that follows. And while sustained, long-term interactions may hold more potential to influence group-based attitudes (Toosi et al. 2012; MacInnis and Page-Gould 2015), these long-term relationships develop out of initial encounters with strangers. Understanding the initial point of contact, then, can shed light on what kinds of interactions are likely to develop into long-term connections.

2.4.2 The Outgroup

Many important social divisions exist in American political and social life, and my goal is not to explore each of them simultaneously. Instead, I explore the political consequences of different kinds of contact across one kind of boundary – race and ethnicity – and look to future research to establish the same patterns with other types of social groups.

There are good theoretical reasons for this focus. Race and ethnicity are enduring and salient features of American society. Additionally, racial and ethnic divisions play an important role in the American *political* system.

A substantial body of research confirms that racial and ethnic attachments influence political attitudes (Kam and Kinder 2012; Bracic, Israel-Trummel, and Shortle 2019), behaviors (Dawson 1995; Leighley and Vedlitz 1999), and critical concepts like partisanship (Abrajano and Hajnal 2015; Mason 2018). Many go as far to say that American politics cannot be understood without incorporating race (King and Smith 2014).

Focusing on race and ethnicity also has practical benefits. Individuals notice and make inferences about race and ethnicity rapidly and without conscious effort. Perceiving racial and ethnic divisions often does not require explicit verbal cues, making such groupings salient in short interactions with outgroup strangers even when race is not explicitly discussed (Macrae and Quadflieg 2010; Bodenhausen, Kang, and Peery 2012). This simplifies the structure of the interactions, makes longer conversations unnecessary to emphasize group membership, and implies that the interactions created in these experiments are comparable to the brief experiences individuals have with outgroup individuals in real settings.

2.4.3 The Conditions

How might intergroup experiences influence political support for outgroups? As noted earlier, contact research does not clearly explain when contact promotes negative and positive reactions to outgroups. There is a nearly infinite set of factors that might influence the outcome of intergroup experiences – the content of these encounters, the motivations that individuals pursue throughout the experience, Allport's four conditions, friendship potential, and more. Manipulating every element at once would be both prohibitively complex and impede theory testing. My approach, then, is to start by more closely considering one of Allport's conditions that has important connections to politics and democratic theory: equal status.

In its original formulation, contact theory suggested that interactions between people from different social groups could be improved by creating a sense of equality between participants within the contact scenario itself (e.g., Allport 1954; Pettigrew 1969; Riordan 1978; Pettigrew 1998). In other words, equal status centers on how contact participants treat each other and present themselves within the contact encounter. This can be contrasted with equal status between people more generally, which requires that participants in contact have, outside of the contact encounter, the same amounts of social, economic, and political power (a particularly difficult task for many of the group divisions in many societies). As already noted, equal status has important links to various theoretical ideas in political science, such as deliberative theories of democracy (S. Chambers 2003; Thompson 2008; Mansbridge et al. 2012).

Early discussions of equal status in contact emphasized that status, especially in intergroup settings, is deeply rooted in expectations about the behavior of others (Riordan 1978). Empirical evaluations of these ideas consistently find that confidence and competence in interacting with other people are important markers of status. Changing the confidence and competence of racial minorities, for example, shifts how influential they are in interactions with White people and how they are perceived (Cohen and Roper 1972; Cohen, Lockheed, and Lohman 1976; Riordan and Ruggiero 1980). Focusing on specific demographic characteristics (like income or social class), on the other hand, is far less effective in influencing status perceptions of racial outgroups (Cohen and Roper 1972; Cohen, Lockheed, and Lohman 1976; Riordan and Ruggiero 1980). While these studies have not been repeated in a more recent context and typically used very small sample sizes, this research suggests that how people communicate and present themselves can serve as an effective and socially important signal of status.

In the experiments that follow, I build on these ideas and manipulate status by focusing on the ease of communication between individuals. By ease of communication, I mean the lack of barriers to understanding the other person in the encounter. In psychology, this concept is called *processing fluency* and refers to the relationship between the difficulty of understanding something (an interaction, image, other stimuli, etc.) and subsequent cognitive, emotional, and interpersonal processes.[4] Based on the level of difficulty in communicating, people form impressions that then influence how they think and act toward the object at hand. This notion of fluency is a basic element of nearly all social and nonsocial experiences (Oppenheimer 2008); psychologists have explored fluency in intergroup interactions (Pearson and Dovidio 2014; Lick and Johnson 2015), judgments (Schwarz 2004), and bias (Rubin, Paolini, and Crisp 2010). Importantly, the consequences of fluency depend on how individuals intuitively interpret their feelings and can vary widely depending on these "naive" explanations.

In the experiments that follow, I vary the ease of communicating by changing various nonverbal components of speech. This involves changing the amount of eye contact, pauses, and body language on the part of the confederate outgroup member. These manipulations come from research on interpersonal interactions, social cognition, and conversational norms about what does and does not promote communication between individuals. As discussed in the following sections, confederate outgroup members vary these

---

[4] I prefer the term ease of communication to prevent confusion with English-language proficiency. At the time of this writing, only one political science study uses this concept and applies it to the structure of media stories (Berinsky and Kinder 2006).

elements without changing the substance of what is said or the setting in which intergroup contact occurs.

I rely on the ease of communications to manipulate equal status perceptions for several reasons. Easier-to-understand encounters promote impressions of similarity, competence, and confidence on the part of the outgroup. These should be associated with an increased impression of the outgroup's status – the outgroup member presents themselves as a confident equal and does not send nonverbal cues about deference or a lack of ability. This manipulation of status avoids many of the issues alternative status manipulations face as they often unintentionally bring in Allport's other conditions (Pettigrew 1969; Riordan 1978). For example, encouraging equal status by assigning individuals to the same task or to explicitly work together combines equal status with cooperation and the pursuit of common goals. This type of confounding prevents researchers from making rigorous conclusions about any of Allport's conditions. Focusing on communication difficulty therefore provides insight into one of the four original conditions suggested by contact theory without this kind of causal muddying and can lay a groundwork for other scholars interested in the criteria proposed by the literature on contact.

As it is a regular feature of all social experiences, examining the difficulty in communicating also does not set up idealized and unachievable forms of intergroup contact. Further, it can be manipulated directly without changing the explicit content or setting of contact; as such, the ease of communication can be changed in isolation, leading to strong causal inferences about this element of intergroup interactions.

Focusing on the ease of communications (instead of the other manipulations of confidence and competence used by early studies of contact) also provides insight into how this condition may lead to more or less outgroup support with its emphasis on people's intuitive explanations. With this in mind, the ease of communications should work as outlined in Figure 1. People first experience the interaction with an outgroup member that varies in its ease of communication (step 1). The ease of communication shifts perceptions of the outgroup member, as shown in step 2. Subsequently, easy-to-understand individuals should prompt a stronger sense of similarity with the larger outgroup (Alter and Oppenheimer 2009; Pearson and Dovidio 2014) and increased perceptions of competence and confidence on the part of the outgroup (Cohen and Roper 1972; Cohen, Lockheed, and Lohman 1976; Riordan and Ruggiero 1980). In contrast, hard-to-understand individuals should be perceived as less similar, less competent, and less confident.

The perceptions from step 2 can then be intuitively explained in ways that lead to different implications for outgroup support, as laid out in step 3. One

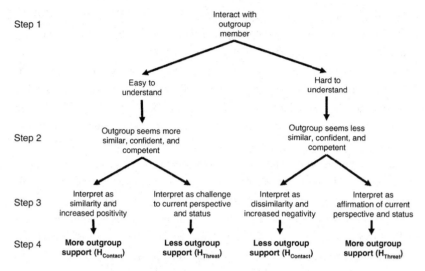

Figure 1 Reactions to the ease of communicating

possible interpretation of these perceptions is that individuals will react to easier communications with more support for the outgroup (see $H_{Contact}$ in step 4). The psychological sensation of easy communications should be more positive than more difficult communications; in these settings many interpret their positivity as reflective of the person being understood (Pearson et al. 2008; Pearson and Dovidio 2014). Easy communications can also indicate that the outgroup is more likeable and less threatening. In a parallel way, harder communications reinforce group differences and are interpreted as signals of group-based divisions. These predictions would support the traditional approach to intergroup contact and discussions of equal status within this literature.

However, close, similar, competent, and confident outgroups need not necessarily promote outgroup support. Easy communications could leave perceptions of other groups unchanged. They may also provoke a sense of threat. Interpreted through a group threat framework, easy communications challenge perceptions of the position of the ingroup relative to other social groups, threaten the status of that ingroup, and create a sense of intergroup anxiety. From a social identity perspective, outgroup similarity can undermine the positive distinctiveness people draw from ingroups, intensifying motivations to favor the ingroup and react against the outgroup (Tajfel 1978; Leonardelli, Pickett, and Brewer 2010; Danyluck and Page-Gould 2018).

This reaction is theoretically linked with the tendency of individuals, especially from majority groups, to respond dramatically to threats to their racial status (Craig and Richeson 2014b; Major, Blodorn, and Blascovich 2016), to react to expectation-defying outgroup individuals with more overall negativity and threat perceptions (Mendes et al. 2007), and to think that an increase in the position and status of one group necessarily comes at the expense of their own (e.g., Meegan 2010; Norton and Sommers 2011; Wilkins and Kaiser 2014; Wilkins et al. 2015). Under these conditions, outgroup support should decrease as feelings of outgroup competition, threat, and group-based anxiety increase (Hajnal 2001; Riek, Mania, and Gaertner 2006; Cuddy, Fiske, and Glick 2008). In contrast, hard-to-understand outgroup members should confirm individuals' expectations and fail to provoke a sense of group- and status-based threat. These predictions are represented in Figure 1 in H_{Threat}. The contact and threat predictions are direct opposites and draw on distinct theories of communication and intergroup relationships. As such, one goal of this research is to evaluate when intergroup experiences create the reactions predicted by contact theory, when they instead generate threat-consistent reactions, and when they fail to change individuals' group-based and political attitudes in either direction.

2.5 Using the Framework

In this Element, I propose a way to study the political consequences of intergroup contact in a manner that addresses the uncertainties in contact research and productively contributes to discussions about the problems of groups in democratic society. Sections 3 and 4 apply the framework from this section, both to illustrate the value of this kind of experimentation and to explore the democratic consequences of intergroup contact. In the sections that follow, I describe the differences between easy and hard-to-understand encounters, outline the experiments in more detail, and test the predictions from Figure 1.

3 Applications in the Lab, Experiment 1

In this section, I describe an experiment that creates intergroup contact between participants and a lab administrator, manipulates the difficulty of understanding the outgroup member in the contact encounter, evaluates both contact and threat-based theories, considers a range of political outcomes, involves a White and non-White sample, and includes measures of decay. As such, this section directly applies the proposed elements from Section 2. The analyses from this experiment indicate that intergroup contact fails to promote understanding between groups even when it is intentionally structured to promote impressions of equal status and easy communications. Further, such equal-status contact promotes a backlash among White subjects, who become less politically supportive of racial minorities.

3.1 Understanding the Effects of Intergroup Contact

As reviewed in Sections 1 and 2, research on intergroup contact presents an uncertain picture of how these kinds of interactions can and cannot produce democratically beneficial outcomes. Understanding the potential of these social encounters, therefore, requires careful research applying the framework from Section 2. Among other things, this entails describing the type of contact under consideration, which elements of contact will be manipulated, and the theoretical perspectives underlying these choices.

For the reasons listed in Section 2, I examine brief interactions with outgroup strangers, a common kind of contact. These social experiences are prominent in American social life: Americans encounter strangers on a regular basis and are also most likely to meet other social groups among those strangers. Yet, they have been understudied by social scientists and contact researchers.

To understand the political consequences of this type of intergroup contact (brief, racial contact between strangers), I examine equal status by randomizing the ease or difficulty of communicating in contact. To reiterate the justifications provided in Section 2, communication difficulty is a ubiquitous feature of all social experiences and can be manipulated directly and separately from the setting, content, or any other part of contact. Further, it has theoretical connections to Allport's condition of equal status.

The ease of communicating also has connections to existing studies of intergroup interactions. Compared to communications among ingroup members, intergroup conversations require more cognitive resources and generate more anxiety (Petronio et al. 1998; Trawalter and Richeson 2008); this is at least partially due to difficulties in communicating. Many forms of contact-based policy interventions deliberately focus on improving communications between groups, suggesting the practical importance of this focus (Martin and Hecht 1994; Walsh 2007; Kirwan Institute for the study of race and ethnicity 2010).

Research in psychology suggests several ways that the ease of communicating can influence the consequences of contact. In social interactions, other individuals can behave in ways that make them easier or harder to understand. This is part of a larger set of experiences people have when encountering stimuli of all types – people, texts, images, etc. When people encounter a stimulus, they form an impression of that thing based on how hard it is to understand. These impressions then color the inferences drawn from the encounter.

As an illustration, consider Figure 2. It shows the same text presented in two ways, with different kinds of contrast and fonts. Someone reading

Example 1	Various kinds of excercise to not promote overall health
Example 2	Various kinds of excercise to not promote overall health

Figure 2 Text example of communication difficulty

a difficult-to-understand font (example 1) will likely, due to the difficulty reading the text, feel a sense of difficulty. They then might attribute these feelings to the reliability or source of the information, rather than size and contrast of the font. In contrast, they will more easily process the text in example 2 even though the information is identical. When the font is easier to read, people should then feel a sense of familiarity and comfort and apply these reactions to the source and content of the message. Importantly, this process works outside of conscious awareness – when individuals are made aware of the source of their feelings, they discount their initial reactions and impressions (Alter and Oppenheimer 2009).

Applying this process to contact, outgroup members who are easier to understand should be perceived as closer to one's self. People, in turn, apply these reactions beyond the specific outgroup individual to the outgroup as a whole (Pettigrew and Tropp 2011, 29).[5] As noted previously, these kinds of outgroup perceptions have a direct connection to Allport's condition of equal status as socially-proximate groups should seem more equal to one's own group than more distant outgroups.

Once individuals experience an easy- or difficult-to-understand form of contact, the ease of communicating could influence intergroup affect and support in different ways. On one hand, people could interpret easy-to-understand encounters with outgroups as indicative of familiarity with that group and respond with more trust. This would lead to increased positivity toward the larger outgroup. More difficulty in communicating, on the other hand, could emphasize group-based differences, more clearly separate the ingroup and outgroup, and bring negative feelings to mind (Pearson et al. 2008).

From this point of view, ease of understanding should promote political support for the outgroup. As outgroup trust and familiarity increase, support for government policies and political actions that benefit those outgroups should also increase (e.g., Gilens 2000; Gibson 2006; Kinder and Kam 2009). I refer to this prediction as $H_{Contact}$ because it shares the same underlying logic as contact research more generally:

---

[5] There are some exceptions – such as when people subtype outgroup members – but contact studies find that in the majority of cases, people generalize their feelings to the larger outgroup. As discussed in the results of this experiment, I do not observe evidence consistent with subtyping.

$H_{Contact}$: *As compared to difficult-to-understand interactions, easy-to-understand intergroup contact should promote more support for policies and political action intended to benefit the relevant outgroup, all else constant.*

However, theories on group threat and stereotypes suggest alternative ways of interpreting the ease of communicating. Easy interactions across group boundaries can make the outgroup feel socially closer to one's own group. In many settings, such a feeling of closeness is perceived as jeopardizing the status of one's own group and prompts more outgroup threat reaction (Craig and Richeson 2014a). Given that people derive a positive sense of uniqueness and self-worth from their ingroups, an increased sense of outgroup similarity can prompt a need to react against the outgroup (Tajfel 1978; Danyluck and Page-Gould 2018). Increasing the ease of communication also makes outgroup members appear more capable and more assertive. This may prompt feelings of hostility and competition with the outgroup, which then may decrease support for actions in favor of that group (Hajnal 2001; Riek, Mania, and Gaertner 2006; Cuddy, Fiske, and Glick 2008). In contrast, more difficult-to-understand outgroup members reduce perceived outgroup threat, as these groups seem less capable than – and more distant from – one's ingroup. This process need not be conscious: easy-to-understand outgroup members can subconsciously challenge the way one sees the world, defy expectations for outgroup behavior, and generate a sense of outgroup threat and anxiety (Mendes et al. 2007). This threat-based reaction should, in turn, reduce outgroup political support, suggesting H_{Threat}:

H_{Threat}: *As compared to difficult-to-understand interactions, easy-to-understand intergroup contact should promote less support for policies and political action in favor of the relevant group, all else constant.*

Social groups are not all interchangeable, and I do not expect members of all kinds of groups to show the trends described in $H_{Contact}$ and H_{Threat} in the same way. Work on contact more generally finds that majority group members respond more strongly to contact (Pettigrew and Tropp 2011). This could be because minority group members have more extensive experience with majority groups than vice versa and thus, any particular social experience should be more influential for majority group members. Further, majority groups have more to lose in terms of status, and majority group members react more readily to outgroup threat (e.g., Ellemers et al. 1992; Bettencourt et al. 2001; Danbold and Huo 2015). This leads to a third hypothesis:

$H_{Majority}$: *As compared to minority group members, majority group members should experience greater effects of the ease of communication, all else constant.*

3.2 Methods, Procedures, and Measures

I conducted a laboratory experiment from November 2016 to June 2017 to test these hypotheses. Subjects came from undergraduate political science courses at a private university in the American Midwest. Table 1 provides demographics on the sample used in this experiment, blocking by White and non-White (as explained shortly). This table indicates that the sample is quite liberal and may be more resistant to feelings of racial threat – previous work indicates that Republicans and conservatives can be more sensitive to these kinds of threats than Democrats and liberals (Jost et al. 2007; Hawley 2011; Hopkins 2014). As a result, I would expect the sample to be predisposed in favor of $H_{Contact}$, rather than H_{Threat}.

The participants first signed up for a time to complete the study through a short survey. This survey included a measure of racial self-identification, which I then used to create intergroup contact. Following this sign-up, each subject came to the lab at their assigned time and had an interaction with an outrace lab administrator who was trained to act in specific ways. I hired six administrators: two females presenting as Black, one male presenting as Black, two females presenting as White, and one male presenting as White.[6] Administrators and subjects were blind to the study's hypotheses.

Table 1 Experiment 1, subject demographics

	Non-White subjects	White subjects
Percent female	61%	49%
Average year in school	Sophomore	Sophomore
Ideology (Extremely liberal– Extremely conservative)	Somewhat liberal	Somewhat liberal
Partisanship (Strong Democrat to Strong Republican)	Not so strong Democrat	Independent-leaning Democrat
Average self-reported importance of racial identity (1–7)	5.2	3.2
Total N	151	259

---

[6] Photos of the administrators can be found in the Online Appendix.

I assigned each subject to a lab session based on their racial self-identification. The design and analyses thus proceeded with a block randomized design, blocking by racial identification into White and non-White groups. Ideally, this study would consider specific non-White racial groups, but the composition of the student sample does not allow for those kinds of comparisons. Non-Latinx White subjects were assigned to sessions with a phenotypically Black administrator. Non-White and Latinx subjects were assigned to sessions with a phenotypically White administrator. Each lab session contained one to five subjects from the same racial group (White or non-White) and one outrace administrator; the typical group consisted of three respondents.

At their assigned time, subjects came to the lab for their experimental session. The administrator then directed each to a separate computer terminal. To prevent spillover between treatments, I randomly assigned all subjects in the same lab session to the same treatment group – minimal, easy-to-understand, and difficult-to-understand interactions. Table 2 presents the different conditions, along with the number of subjects assigned to each.

In conditions C1, C2, C4, and C5, the administrator spoke briefly with each participant individually – asking the participant's name, giving a brief introduction to the study, and clarifying some logistical points. The whole experience lasted about two to three minutes and made no explicit mention of race or racial groups. In this encounter, the administrator gave a racially-stereotypical name – Eboni or Jabari for Black administrators and Shelbi or Dalton for White administrators.[7] Administrators also indicated that they were from a city overwhelmingly composed of their racial group, but they did not mention the racial composition of that city. These cues, along with the

Table 2 Experiment 1 conditions

	Administrator	
Ease or difficulty	*Black administrator, White subjects*	*White administrator, non-White subjects*
Easy-to-understand	C1: Black, easy interaction (91)	C4: White, easy interaction (59)
Difficult-to-understand	C2: Black, difficult interaction (90)	C5: White, difficult interaction (54)
Minimal interaction	C3: Black, minimal interaction (78)	C6: White, minimal interaction (36)

---

[7] These names were selected as being highly correlated with the gender-racial combinations used in the experiment based on a census of names and demographic traits from the state of Florida.

appearance of the administrators, reinforced the group division between the subject and the administrator.

Although administrators used the same script in the contact conditions, the conversations differed in how easy they were to understand. For the subjects in C1 and C4, the administrator created an easy-to-understand interaction in four ways, as illustrated in Table 3. First, the administrator directly faced the subject, a type of body language that is rapidly noticed and important to interpersonal interactions (Perrett et al. 1985; Nummenmaa and Calder 2009). Second, the administrator made regular eye contact with the subject, which facilitates social experiences. It is reflexively noticed in social interactions (Emery 2000; Shepherd 2010) and rapidly engages the social structures of the brain (Senju and Johnson 2009). Third, the administrator paused no more than once. Pauses directly introduce a barrier in speech and listening, influencing perceptions of others and their social groups (Pearson et al. 2008; Koudenburg, Postmes, and Gordijn 2013). Finally, the administrator spoke with a natural, expressive tone. This kind of tone, as compared to monotone, helps individuals interpret the meaning of ambiguous words and better understand emotions (Nygaard and Lunders 2002; Nygaard and Queen 2008).

In the difficult-to-understand conditions (C2 and C5), the administrator faced away from the subjects, made eye contact only once during the conversation, paused between five and seven times for several seconds, and spoke in monotone. These elements served as the opposites of those in the easy-to-understand experiences. Several independent pilot tests and the results of the experiments in Section 4 suggest that subjects perceive these manipulations as expected – the easy-to-understand outgroup member is rated as easier to understand, more similar to the subject, warmer, and more competent.

A comparison of the easy and difficult conditions is the key test for the hypotheses. However, these contrasts do not indicate which of the two has

Table 3 Ease of communication manipulations

Easy-to-understand	Hard-to-understand
Administrator directly faced subject with body and face	Administrator faced away from subject
Administrator made eye contact at least four times	Administrator made eye contact only once during the conversation
Administrator paused briefly only once	Administrator paused five to seven times for several seconds each time
Administrator spoke in a natural, expressive vocal tone	Administrator spoke in monotone

a larger relative effect compared to no interaction at all. I thus included the minimal interaction conditions (C3 and C6), where the administrator simply indicated that the subject should begin the survey without an extended conversation. These conditions serve as a useful empirical comparison point of mere exposure instead of intergroup contact.

After the treatment, subjects completed a survey that measured their political support for the outgroup in the contact. Subjects first completed items about government action on behalf of White Americans, racial minorities, Muslims, and LGBT individuals. The last two groups helped mask the purpose of the experiment and explore whether these interactions influence support for groups unconnected to the outgroup in the interaction. The first question asked subjects to report how much they thought the "federal government should do to make sure members of the following groups are treated fairly when it comes to education and employment opportunities"; answer choices ranged from nothing at all (1) to a great deal (7). Participants then responded to a similar question about fair treatment in the criminal justice system. The last policy item asked subjects to indicate their support or opposition to "college admissions programs that give preferential treatment to members of that group."[8] These items represent three areas where one might expect group-based considerations to be influential (Bobo 2000; Gilens 2000).

After these items, subjects indicated whether they would support or oppose two separate demonstrations: one "advocating for greater government protection for racial minorities" and the other "advocating that affirmative action disadvantages deserving Whites."[9] For each, subjects indicated their support or opposition to the demonstration under four circumstances: when it took place at the university, when it blocked traffic, when it clashed with local police, and when it raised money for a local charity. I intentionally chose these more concrete tolerance judgments over more generic measures of political tolerance, as people tend to report agreement with the values of tolerance while holding a number of specific intolerant beliefs (e.g., Gibson 2013). These items also reduce social desirability problems since they allow individuals to express opposition toward the demonstration for ostensibly non-racial reasons. Participants then completed a few more items about both kinds of demonstrations (not analyzed here), perceptions of discrimination, and impressions of the administrator.

After completing these items, participants left the lab. About ten days later, participants completed a post-lab survey, which included the main outcomes

---

[8] For all items, subjects answered questions about outgroups and then the ingroup.
[9] Subjects answered questions about outgroups first.

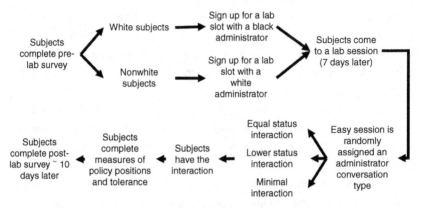

Figure 3 Experiment 1 design

from the experiment and a debrief. At this point, their participation was complete. Figure 3 summarizes this design.

3.3 Results

Regardless of treatment assignment, most subjects reported favorable attitudes toward racial minorities. Support for outgroup demonstrations varies with the description of the demonstration – support increases when the demonstration raises money for charity and falls when it clashes with police (see Table 4).

Testing the hypotheses presented earlier relies on a technique called nonparametric combination (NPC). This method is a type of permutation test that allows researchers to test hypotheses on sets of related dependent variables while accounting for the relationships between those variables. It does so in a way that is not reliant on modeling assumptions or various kinds of approximations and can be especially useful in circumstances with low statistical power. Ultimately, this method produces a p-value on estimated treatment effects for each variable and then a global p-value. This global p-value indicates the likelihood of observing the results across all of the dependent variables under a sharp null hypothesis of no effect (for more details, see Pesarin and Salmaso 2010; Caughey, Dafoe, and Seawright 2017). In the context of this experiment, NPC allows the analyses to consider the measures of outgroup political support individually and in a combined way. In the Online Appendix, I present secondary analyses that implement other techniques (such as randomization inference, t-tests, bootstrapping, etc.) to ensure the analytic choice of NPC does not drive the results and conclusions that follow.

Table 4 gives the means and standard errors of these dependent variables, broken out by the racial blocking and treatment groups. Figure 4 displays the

Table 4 Experiment 1, means by treatment conditions within each racial block

	NON-WHITE SUBJECTS						WHITE SUBJECTS					
	Minimal		Easy-to-understand		Difficult-to-understand		Minimal		Easy-to-understand		Difficult-to-understand	
	Mean	SE	Mean	SE	Mean	SE	Mean	SE	Mean	SE	Mean	SE
Criminal justice	6.444	0.096	6.661	0.075	6.685	0.103	6.564	0.086	6.176	0.081	6.533	0.106
Equal opportunity	5.056	0.192	4.559	0.145	4.500	0.162	5.179	0.173	4.714	0.164	5.033	0.157
Preferential treatment	3.806	0.107	3.864	0.086	3.722	0.091	2.949	0.099	2.802	0.092	3.011	0.091
Demonstration	2.778	0.201	2.237	0.170	2.463	0.192	5.756	0.207	5.462	0.179	5.989	0.186
Demonstration blocking traffic	2.194	0.194	1.814	0.159	1.722	0.181	4.397	0.189	4.000	0.170	4.656	0.180
Demonstration clashing with police	1.583	0.159	1.644	0.148	1.463	0.149	3.269	0.170	3.275	0.148	3.300	0.149
Demonstration raising money for charity	3.361	0.195	2.898	0.160	3.056	0.178	6.359	0.195	6.022	0.167	6.467	0.176

Notes: Responses ranged from 1 to 7, with 1 indicating the lowest support for the outgroup and 7 the highest. The only exception is preferential treatment, which ranged from 1 (lowest support) to 5 (most support).

comparisons between the easy- and hard-to-understand groups for both White and non-White subjects, showing the absolute change, the percent change, the associated p-value on the difference between the easy- and hard-to-understand groups, and the effect size of this difference (Hedges' g – this is a version of Cohen's d, adjusted for smaller sample sizes). In addition, the top of each pane of the graph presents the global p-value for the NPC analysis.

When White subjects have easy-to-understand outrace experiences, they report lower support for government and political action on behalf of racial minorities. The overall p-value on this treatment effect is highly significant (p=0.01), indicating that it would be extremely unlikely to observe these differences if support for racial outgroups was the same in both the easy and hard conditions. Turning to specific dependent variables, support for government action in the realm of criminal justice reliably decreases in response to easy-to-understand outgroup members: the treatment results in a 6 percent change in support for government action in this area. Support for the demonstrations responds to the treatment similarly except for demonstrations clashing with police. The clashing with police item may represent a circumstance where subjects' views are more rigid.[10] In every case, I fail to observe any reactions to contact that are consistent with the idea that these experiences

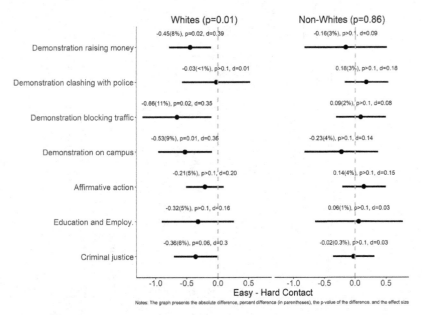

Figure 4 Experiment 1 results

---

should prompt more support for outgroups ($H_{Contact}$). For four out of the seven outcomes, the comparisons support H_{Threat}. For two of the remaining outcomes (equality in education and employment and affirmative action), differences are in the correct direction for H_{Threat} but fall short of statistical significance.

The threat-consistent patterns shown in Figure 4 could be from a reduction of support from the easy-to-understand form of contact or a boost in support from the hard-to-understand interaction. Considering the minimal condition helps to evaluate these two possibilities. NPC analyses suggest that the hard-to-understand form of contact is never statistically distinct from the minimal condition (p-values range from 0.24 to 0.91; global p-value is 0.75). The easy-to-understand form of contact, on the other hand, does show reduced levels of support for racial minorities in comparison to the minimal group. While these results are not as stark as the comparison between the hard and easy forms of contact (p-values range from 0.04 to ~1; global p-value is 0.1), the data continue to provide no evidence for the idea that the hard-to-understand conditions *increase* political support for outgroups.

As shown by the non-White panel of Figure 4, the treatments never have an effect for non-White subjects. The global p-value is quite large (p=0.85), failing to provide evidence against the null hypothesis of no treatment effect. Individual p-values never approach statistical significance and vary in terms of their direction. This is another failure to find any support for $H_{Contact}$. These results also indicate strong support for $H_{Majority}$, which predicted that the effects should be more pronounced for White subjects. It also confirms prior studies that suggest that advantaged and disadvantaged groups respond differently to contact experiences.

The design of the experiment also allows for an examination of these effects over time. Subjects were all recontacted seven to ten days after the interactions in the lab, and this recontact reassessed the measures of outgroup support displayed in Figure 4. NPC analyses of these recontact measures for White subjects (the group showing effects in the lab) indicates that the treatments no longer have an effect after seven to ten days – the global p-value is 0.29, failing to provide evidence against the null hypothesis of no treatment effects. The treatment effects present in the lab seem to disappear entirely when subjects are reinterviewed about a week later.

To support this conclusion, I also consider change over time in both the easy- and hard-to-understand groups. Figure 5 displays this differences-in-differences approach, which compares the change from the lab to recontact across the easy- and hard-to-understand treatment conditions. In this graph, more positive numbers mean a higher increase in the variable in the easy-to-understand group – in

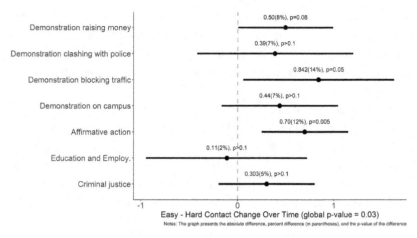

Figure 5 Experiment 1, over time results

other words, a fading of treatment effects over time. These analyses and the global NPC p-value (p=0.03) suggest that the negative response to the easy-to-understand outgroup member weakens over time, and further comparisons suggest that these changes are not the result of general attitude instability. What continues to be evident from these findings, however, is that contact produces no increase in outgroup support, either immediately after or several days removed from the experience.

To confirm these analyses, I conducted a series of robustness checks. Alternative methods of analysis like randomization inference and bootstrapping lead to the same conclusions as the NPC method. Consideration of administrator-specific effects finds that individual administrators do not moderate nor eliminate the treatment effect. Incorporating gender match between the subject and administrator leads to the same conclusions. The results also do not depend on when (temporally) the subject completed the study in the lab. The Online Appendix contains more details on these analyses.

As noted, these findings show no support for $H_{Contact}$ and multiple instances supporting the threat-based propositions of H_{Threat}. However, due to concerns about priming threat-based attitudes and the need to keep the survey instrument brief, the experiment did not include any direct measures of racial or status threat. The experiment did include items that can be used to rule out four alternative explanations of the findings that are distinct from the threat-based mechanism in H_{Threat}. These alternative explanations are: (1) increased preferences for the ingroup in the easy-to-understand condition, (2) increased antipathy for only the specific outgroup member, (3) prompting a general sense of negativity instead of group-specific threat, and (4) generating empathy in the hard-to-understand condition rather than threat in the easy-to-understand group. I discuss each of these explanations in turn.

The first alternative explanation for these results is that the conversations prompt subjects' preferences for their own racial group rather than a sense of increased negativity toward and threat from the outgroup. Ingroup love and outgroup denigration are conceptually distinct phenomena, operate through different processes, result in different kinds of intergroup conflict, and have different normative implications (Brewer 1999; Halevy, Weisel, and Bornstein 2012; Greenwald and Pettigrew 2014). If the treatments prompt more ingroup favoritism (rather than outgroup antipathy), subjects may simply be expressing stronger preferences for their own group when they report lower levels of support for the outgroup. However, the data from the experiment does not support this conclusion. The experiment included measures of support for one's own group, and White subjects do not display stronger preferences for their own racial group in the easy-to-understand condition (global p-value for inrace items of 0.39; each individual item is also statistically insignificant). This finding strongly undermines the claim that the easy-to-understand condition generated a stronger preference for the ingroup and not a stronger sense of outgroup antipathy, especially when combined with the design components that prime the racial identity of the outgroup member (rather than the subjects' racial identity).

The second alternative explanation is that subjects are merely expressing increased negativity toward the *specific* outgroup member rather than the outgroup as a whole. This suggestion is not supported by the vast majority of contact research by either advocates or skeptics of intergroup contact, which find broad support for the idea that people easily make leaps from outgroup individuals to the outgroup as a whole (e.g., Pettigrew and Tropp 2011). It would be possible, though, if respondents engage in a form of subtyping where they conclude the outgroup member is not representative of the larger group and, therefore, they should not change their views of the group as a result of anything the outgroup member does (see, for example, Park, Wolsko, and Judd 2001; Richards and Hewstone 2001). The data from the experiment do not support this kind of subtyping process – subjects were asked how much the outgroup member seemed to be representative of their racial group. On this item there are no reliable differences between the two treatment groups (p=0.53), challenging the idea that subjects are expressing more negative attitudes about the individual rather than the larger outgroup.

The third alternative explanation, that the easy-to-understand treatments prompt a general sense of negativity rather than an outgroup-specific reaction, is also not supported by the data. In addition to the racial group outcomes, the survey also included questions about Muslims and LGBT communities. These two groups are typically not connected to the outgroups involved in the interaction. If the easy-to-understand administrator creates an overall nega- tivity (due to being forced to engage with the administrator in a more involved way, for example), I would expect this negativity to influence the Muslim and LGBT outcomes in addition to the questions about racial minor- ities. The data do not support this proposition – subjects' attitudes on the Muslim and LGBT items in the easy- and hard-to-understand groups are not reliably different (global, NPC p-value of 0.25). The effects of the treatments seem specific to racial minorities.

The final alternative explanation proposes that the results described previ- ously could be produced by increased empathy in the hard-to-understand condition without an increased amount of threat in the easy-to-understand condition. This would produce the same empirical findings but presumably would work through a very different process. The minimal interaction condition becomes key here, as it allows me to evaluate whether the hard-to-understand group is more positive than the minimal group (suggesting the empathy pro- cess), whether the easy-to-understand group is more negative than the minimal group (suggesting the threat process), or some combination of the two (suggest- ing a more complex causal story). If this were true, I would also expect that empathy to influence perceptions of discrimination faced by the racial group in question.

As with the other two explanations, the data do not support this alternative set of predictions. The results displayed in Table 4 and reported earlier support the threat-based mechanism over the empathy theory: the minimal condition is never statistically different from the hard-to-understand group (global p-value of 0.75). The easy-to-understand condition, on the other hand, is statistically different from the minimal group, both on the global NPC p-value (p=0.10) and several individual dependent variables. This, combined with the fact that perceptions of discrimination are not statistically different between the treat- ment conditions (p=0.47), suggests further support for the theory behind H_{Threat} instead of these alternatives.

3.4 Discussion

This experiment suggests that common social experiences with outgroup mem- bers may not generate the outcomes hoped for by democratic theorists. In no case do I observe the pro-outgroup changes promoted by contact theory. Instead, increased perceptions of outgroup confidence, competence, and simi- larity can lower political support for outgroups.

The implications of these findings are democratically and normatively troubling. Less competent outgroup members who avoid extensive intergroup interactions may avoid the potential costs of contact, but compelling minorities to assume a deferential or avoidant attitude is rife with other normative problems. To the extent that theories of deliberative democracy advocate for easy-to-understand interactions (Sanders 1997; Thompson 2008), they might unintentionally exacerbate the very problems they hope to address.

Like all research, these findings are subject to limitations. The treatments used here examined interracial encounters – specifically interactions between White and Black individuals and non-White and White individuals. Further work is needed to determine how the findings here operate with other group boundaries, such as national, religious, or ethnic divisions. In a related way, the treatments only influenced White subjects. If, as $H_{Majority}$ suggests, different levels of experience with outrace individuals explains this, we would expect a weaker treatment effect among White people who have more previous contact with Black individuals. This is confirmed in these data – White subjects with high amounts of previous contact with Black people do not show threat-based reactions to contact.[11] More study of majority group members with different outgroup experiences would help specify precisely when and how these effects work. The heterogeneity of the group "non-Whites" may also be responsible for the failure to find treatment effects among that subset of subjects. Future studies should intentionally study specific non-White racial groups to clarify the results presented here and adjudicate between these possibilities.

Two other elements of the study are worth noting. This study took place with student subjects in a lab setting. While these types of samples can be reliably used to make valid causal inferences (Druckman and Kam 2011), they may involve subjects who are generally more open to the effects of contact, as they typically have more flexible political and social attitudes. Generalizing these findings therefore requires repeating the approach used here with nonstudent samples in more naturalistic contexts.[12] Additionally, the nature of the sample did not allow people to easily opt in and out of contact, leaving unexplored the factors that encourage people to be more or less willing to engage in these kinds of contact experiences.

Despite these limits, this experiment has key implications for the role of contact in democratic society, contact research more generally, and the broader framework presented in Section 2. With regards to the role of contact in democracy, this study suggests that this form of intergroup contact does not promote group-based

---

[11] More details can be found in the Online Appendix.

[12] To the extent that students have larger numbers of racial outgroups in their social networks, these findings would understate the actual impact of interactions with outgroup strangers.

harmony and understanding. In several circumstances, intergroup contact can undermine, rather than bolster, support for outgroups. Further, these patterns are true even when contact is structured to produce easier communications between groups. This section gives additional support to the concern raised by others that social scientists still know little about precisely when contact does and does not address group differences (Paluck, Green, and Green 2018).

In terms of the larger framework presented in Section 2, this experiment demonstrates the importance of the approach advocated for in this Element. By implementing an experiment with controlled, researcher-created contact, the results can speak to the specific feature of contact under consideration (ease of communication) rather than some potential confounder. In a similar way, the experiment can make conclusions about contact directly, without the issues entailed in self-reported contact. The experiment also incorporates multiple theoretical perspectives, as is evidenced by the distinct hypotheses derived from contact theory ($H_{Contact}$) and group-threat theory (H_{Threat}). Additionally, the experiment contains various measures of policy positions, items about ingroup and outgroup attitudes, and measures referring to groups not involved in the contact experience, allowing the experimenter to rule out competing predictions and uncover a more complete picture of the results of contact. Finally, the experiment presented here was intentionally designed with some key generalization elements in mind: subjects were recontacted after the contact experience and the experiment was designed with blocking to make inferences about White and non-White individuals.

With reference to generalization, there are several ways that this experiment should be expanded. One key aspect of generalization is considering how these results differ with different kinds of samples and in different contexts; a single experiment in a single setting cannot address this point. This is especially important given the concerns about the samples commonly used in contact research (e.g., Paluck, Green, and Green 2018). Additionally, generalizing involves considering other group dimensions to demonstrate that the experiment discussed in this section represents a broader group tendency instead of some-thing specific to the relationship between Black and White Americans. Finally, these experiments cannot speak at all to the role of preexisting attitudes about groups nor the way that people choose to opt in and out of intergroup contact; both points are important elements of social group behavior in the real world.

4 Three Experimental Extensions

To replicate the findings from the first experiment and address the questions about generalizability raised in the previous section, I conducted three additional experiments on the political consequences of intergroup contact. These studies all apply the framework from Section 2, manipulate the same elements of contact as experiment 1, and utilize different samples at different points in time. Experiment 2, conducted in suburban neighborhoods and transit centers, involved Latinx pollsters speaking to non-Latinx White individuals. Experiments 3 and 4, in contrast, took place online and used videos of outgroup members to simulate contact between Black and White individuals. Additional details on each study can be found in the Online Appendix.

Across these experiments, I find that while easy-to-understand, equal-status contact can improve interpersonal impressions of outgroup members, it does not increase political support for corresponding groups. In some circumstances, the backlash from Section 3 reemerges. These findings are not contingent on individuals' preexisting racial attitudes nor on other attributes of the outgroup member – with striking consistency, I fail to find one circumstance where easy-to-understand, equal-status contact promotes more political support for racial and ethnic outgroups.

4.1 Orientation of the Experiments

The rest of this section describes three separate experiments, each exploring the empirical results discussed in Section 3 and further applying the framework from Section 2. All three create contact experiences for participants in the studies, draw from the same foundation in psychological research on the ease of communications, focus on brief contact with an outgroup stranger, and look to confirm a lack of support for $H_{Contact}$ and the support for H_{Threat}.

Experiment 1 also found support for $H_{Majority}$, the proposition that contact should have stronger effects for majority groups' political support for minority groups than vice versa. In recognition of this finding, the experiments described in this section focus on White people. This choice aligns with the practices in much of the research on contact and intergroup dynamics, although it highlights the need for work that considers the political consequences of intergroup contact for minority and disadvantaged groups (for a discussion on these points, see Saguy et al. 2009; Saguy and Chernyak-Hai 2012).

4.2 Experiment 2: Contact in the Suburbs

The previous section provided a first test of $H_{Contact}$ and H_{Threat} regarding the consequences of easy- and difficult-to-understand intergroup contact. That experiment, however, leaves many issues unresolved, including how the findings extend to other settings, whether reactions to easy- and hard-to-understand interactions spill over into attitudes about related groups (e.g., contact with

Latinx individuals influencing attitudes toward immigrants), and the way individuals self-select into or out of these types of experiences.

To address these points, I carried out a field experiment in the summer of 2017 involving interactions between Latinx pollsters and non-Latinx adults. As with experiment 1, pollsters delivered a set script to participants in ways that increased or decreased the ease of communication. This second study also incorporated two new components. First, it included measures about an outgroup many Americans linked to Latinx people (immigrants) to explore how these interactions affect support for related social groups. Second, the design of this experiment added an additional measure to explore why people choose to engage or disengage from these experiences – individuals' willingness to participate in outgroup interactions in the first place. Here I find that individuals also appear more willing to interact with outgroup members who are more similar to them; however, I find no support for the idea that easier-to-understand contact generates more support for outgroups (and observe some examples of a backlash). Intergroup contact also influences attitudes toward related outgroups not involved in the contact experience, broadening the scope of contact's effects.

4.2.1 Theoretical Additions

In addition to increased generalizability from using a different sample in a different setting, this experiment has two other contributions. First, the previous section found that brief, intergroup contact failed to influence attitudes toward one's own group and groups unrelated to the outgroup member. How, though, do political attitudes toward *related* outgroups change as a result of intergroup contact?

Psychological theories propose that priming one attitude also activates similar, related constructs. Ideas in memory and in the mind exist in connected networks, with relationships between ideas that facilitate or impede mental activation (e.g., Schröder and Thagard 2013). Additionally, individuals are prone to a number of cognitive biases that prompt them to use accessible information to make judgments, even when that information is not strictly relevant (Tversky and Kahneman 1974; Zaller and Feldman 1992). Taken together, these factors suggest that experiences with a specific outgroup could influence evaluations of a related outgroup, as individuals use the information from the experience in expressing their attitudes toward the second group. This is likely to occur if different groups have high amounts of overlap in membership or if media/social messages often draw connections between two groups. These processes lead to $H_{Spillover}$:

$H_{Spillover}$: *The effects described in $H_{Contact}$ and H_{Threat} should also occur for outgroups related to the group involved in the interpersonal interaction.*

Another crucial question in contact research is how different characteristics of the outgroup member motivate or discourage individuals to engage in these interactions in the first place. The decision to engage with an outgroup member precedes the actual communications; understanding this point helps to contextualize these theories and consider how they apply in more realistic social experiences. Experiment 1 used a captive audience – that is, subjects who could not easily opt out of contact – and cannot speak to this question.

Individuals are generally more willing to cooperate with ingroup members than outgroup members, likely due to factors like greater familiarity, trust, and similarity (Brewer 1999; Balliet, Wu, and De Dreu 2014). A robust literature on interviewer effects comes to similar conclusions, finding that increased similarity between individuals promotes cooperation with an interviewer (e.g., Durrant et al. 2010). These literatures indicate that different kinds of outgroup members should prompt different amounts of interaction. When outgroup members are perceived as more similar to one's own group, individuals will be more likely to initiate an interaction with them, leading to H_{Choice}:

H_{Choice}: *Subjects will be more willing to engage in an intergroup experience with a more similar, as opposed to less similar, outgroup member.*

There is a tension between H_{Threat} and H_{Choice}. While similarity on the part of an outgroup member may prompt more intergroup interaction, similarity can fail to improve contact's consequences and, under certain conditions, generate a sense of intergroup threat. This highlights the challenge of addressing group boundaries through social experiences – the strategies that increase interpersonal engagement across groups may fail to weaken or even increase barriers to resolving group divisions.

4.2.2 Design

To evaluate these hypotheses, I conducted a field experiment in several Midwestern suburban towns in the summer of 2017. To create intergroup contact, I recruited six individuals who self-identified as Latinx[13] and sent them to conduct a survey in areas with few Latinx residents, per the 2010 Census. Table 5 gives the demographic breakdown of the sample in this experiment.

I focus on Latinx people as the outgroup for three main reasons. First, Latinx people are the largest ethnic/racial minority group in the United States, and the number of Latinx individuals in the United States has rapidly increased since the 1980s. Second, Latinx people are a politically important group: a significant

---

[13] Focus groups confirmed that these pollsters were perceived as Latino or Latina. Images of the pollsters can be found in the Online Appendix.

Table 5 Experiment 2 demographic information

Percent Female	52%
Percent White	76%
Average Party Identification	Independent-leaning Democrat
Average Age	49.6
Average Income	Between $100,000 and $199,999
Average Education	4-year degree
N	161

amount of political science research examines the larger political effects Latinx individuals have on American politics (e.g., Oliver 2010; Enos 2014; Abrajano and Hajnal 2015), and Latinx people are frequently mentioned in discussions of elections and campaigns as an important electoral group (e.g., Krogstad and Lopez 2016; Steakin and Scott 2019). Third, emphasizing Latinx ethnicity helps evaluate whether the results of experiment 1 apply only to differences between Black and White Americans or speak also to other racial and ethnic divisions.

The Latinx pollsters were sent to neighborhoods and transit stations. They approached individuals in these areas, introduced themselves using a stereotypical Latinx name, and invited people to speak briefly with them and complete a five-minute survey. For male-presenting pollsters, this name was Alejandro. For female-presenting pollsters, the name was Alejandra. These names were selected as they have a high frequency in middle-class Latinx populations in the United States.[14] This stage of the experiment, when subjects opt in or out of the study, provides a measure of engagement with the outgroup member and an explicit test of H_{Choice}.

Subjects who agreed to have the conversation and complete the survey read a consent form and spoke with the pollster for about two to three minutes. They then answered a series of survey questions about attitudes and tolerance for two groups, Latinx people and immigrants. This survey was completed on a tablet and away from the view of the pollster to address social desirability concerns. Following this survey, subjects were debriefed, thanked, and their participation was complete.

4.2.3 Treatments

The experiment includes two sets of treatments. After agreeing to participate, subjects had one of two possible interactions with the pollster, as determined by random assignment: pollsters either created a difficult-to-understand or an easy-to-understand experience. As in experiment 1, the same script was used in each kind of treatment condition, and pollsters created an easy-to-understand

---

[14] These names were selected using the same Florida census of names as in experiment 1.

interaction in the four ways discussed earlier. First, pollsters directly faced the subject. Second, pollsters made eye contact with the subject at least four times throughout the conversation. Third, pollsters paused no more than once in the interaction and only briefly. Fourth, pollsters spoke with a natural, expressive tone. The difficult-to-understand condition differed in the same nonverbal elements: pollsters faced away from the subjects, made eye contact only once during the conversation, paused between five and seven times for several seconds, and spoke in monotone. In total, the conversations took about two to three minutes.

Pollsters were also randomly assigned to speak with either a Spanish-speaking accent or in unaccented English.[15] While this accent was not explicitly explained to subjects, accents lead to assumptions about shared nationality, English-speaking ability, foreignness, and stigma more generally (Gluszek and Dovidio 2010). In this specific circumstance, accents also indicate further social distance from the respondent's own nationality group and the potential for a more jarring social experience. This treatment thus evaluates H_{Choice} by presenting subjects with the choice to interact with outgroup members with different levels of similarity. Pollsters used the same accent throughout the whole interaction, from the moment they first approached the subject until they concluded the interview. This design creates four conditions, presented in Table 6.

4.2.4 Measures

Two types of data were collected in this study. If the individual declined to participate, the pollster recorded their estimates of the individual's gender, approximate age, and race (White or non-White). If the individual agreed to participate, they spoke with the pollster and then completed a series of survey items after the conversation. Subjects first completed feeling thermometer items about Latinx people and immigrants. A series of Latinx-focused items then followed. Subjects indicated whether they thought Latinx people had too little or too much influence in American politics, whether they favored or opposed

Table 6 Experiment 2, experimental conditions

	Accent	
Ease of communicating	Unaccented	Accented
Easy-to-understand	C1: N=42	C3: N=25
Difficult-to-understand	C2: N=46	C4: N=28

---

[15] The same pollsters collected data speaking with an accent and without.

university affirmative action programs targeted at Latinx people, and their support or opposition for a demonstration advocating for government policies helping Latinx people.[16] The demonstration item also has variations: the demonstration either took place in their community, blocked traffic in front of their home, resulted in conflict with local police, or raised money for a local charity.

Participants next completed a series of similar items about immigrants, a group closely related to Latinxs. They first indicated whether they thought the current level of legal immigration should be decreased, kept the same, or increased. They then stated whether they thought legal immigrants should be eligible for "services like Medicaid or welfare on the same basis as US citizens." Following this item, they indicated support or opposition for a demonstration "advocating for more government policies that help recent immigrants" with the same set of conditions as the pro-Latinx demonstration.

Subjects then answered a set of demographic questions. These included items about subjects' racial and ethnic identification(s), the importance of that identity, citizenship status, the importance of that citizenship to them, and subjects' typical amount of contact with other racial and ethnic groups. The survey concluded with a series of manipulation check items. All subjects were then debriefed about the experiment. At this point, the pollster recorded how much they felt the subject was paying attention during the conversation as an additional data quality check.

4.2.5 Results

Table 6 lists the sample size for each condition and illustrates the smaller sample size for the accented conditions (C3 and C4).[17] The response rate for the unaccented conditions was 31.4 percent; for the accented conditions it was 23.7 percent. At this stage of the experiment, subjects had only been exposed to the pollster's accent but not to barriers in communication (e.g., pauses, eye contact, etc.). Even given this minor difference between the conditions, the difference between the response rates to the accented and unaccented groups is large, statistically significant (0.08, p=0.053), and unrelated to subjects' age, gender, or race. It is also not driven by any individual pollster or location.[18] This suggests that individuals are less willing to engage with an outgroup member

---

[16] The question itself used the term "Latinos" to avoid confusion among subjects about the more uncommon term "Latinxs."

[17] In the following results, the sample excludes Latinx individuals and noncitizens (very few of whom took the survey). Examining the full sample does not produce different conclusions.

[18] These analyses use logistic regression. Clustering by location leads to similar conclusions, with a one-sided p-value of 0.07.

speaking with an accent, even when the other attributes of the individual are held constant, supporting H_{Choice}.

Due to the low sample size in C3 and C4, the analyses that follow focus on the unaccented conditions (C1 and C2). Even these conditions have a limited sample size (N=88). Assuming the conventional levels of power and statistical significance (0.8 and 0.05 respectively), comparisons of C1 to C2 can only detect large effect sizes. For comparisons between C3 and C4, the effect sizes would need to be almost implausibly large, and I therefore do not analyze the accented conditions.

Figure 6 presents differences in levels of support for Latinx people in C1 and C2 on the policy and demonstration items. In this figure, for the ease of presentation, the tolerance items are combined into a single index (α= 0.84); looking at individual tolerance items does not change these conclusions. As in experiment 1, I rely on nonparametric combination analyses (NPC) to estimate the p-values for each dependent variable and the combined set of measures. The results are consistent with the support for H_{Threat} found in experiment 1. The differences in Figure 6 again provide no support for the contact hypothesis and some limited evidence for the threat-based hypothesis. Only the Latinx influence item approaches reliable levels of statistical significance (p=0.03, two-tailed). The global p-value of 0.23 indicates that there does not seem to be a consistent effect across all of these dependent variables.

These conclusions are robust in several ways. Using alternative methods of analysis (such as randomized inference, t-tests, and bootstrapped analyses)

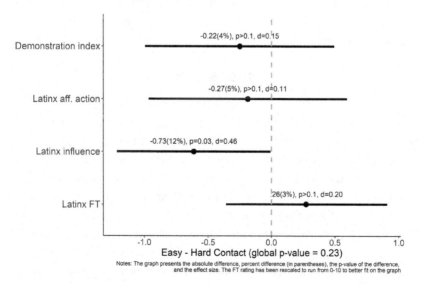

Figure 6 Experiment 2 results, Latinx items

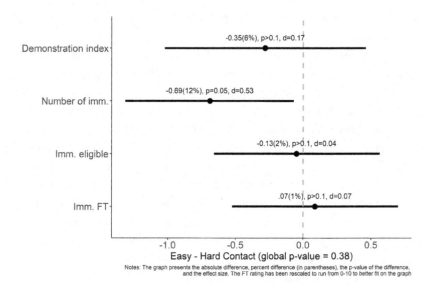

Figure 7 Experiment 2 results, immigrant items

leads to the same conclusions. The observed patterns also are not explained by different kinds of location. Additionally, controlling for pollster gender does not change the patterns presented in Figure 6.

I also find some support for $H_{Spillover}$, that these interactions should influence evaluations of immigrants. Figure 7 graphically presents the differences in the means across treatment groups for each variable. Subjects in the easy condition preferred a lower level of immigration than in the hard condition. On the other items and global p-value, treatment differences fall short of statistical significance.

4.2.6 Discussion

In summary, these data fail to support $H_{Contact}$, just as in the first experiment. They do suggest some support for H_{Threat}, $H_{Spillover}$, and H_{Choice}. When presented with a Latinx pollster who was more difficult to understand (due to an accent), fewer individuals opted into the contact experience. Among those who agreed to engage with an outgroup member, support for Latinx people either did not change depending on the form of contact or decreased. On two specific items – those referring to the influence of Latinx people in the United States and respondents' preferred levels of immigration – subjects expressed less support for Latinx people after having an easy-to-understand contact experience with a Latinx pollster. The change in immigration preferences is notable, as the pollsters explicitly described themselves as American citizens. The results consistent with H_{Threat} are more tenuous here than in experiment 1, perhaps due to differences in the sample size, sample composition, or location. However, once again, I observe a robust, consistent *lack* of support for $H_{Contact}$.

4.3 Experiment 3: Survey Experiment, Bovitz Version

Experiment 2 demonstrates the importance of thinking about generalization when conducting contact experiences, both in terms of clear and more muddled results. However, experiment 2 used a small sample in a restricted geographic area – how do results from experiments 1 and 2 hold up with a more geographically and socially diverse set of American Whites? More centrally, experiment 2 allowed individuals to opt into and out of contact but only observed the attitudes of those who chose to interact with the outgroup member. How might those who rejected the Latinx pollster respond to contact? Previous work stresses the importance of examining these kinds of dynamics to improve the internal and external validity of social science experiments (Gaines and Kuklinski 2011; Arceneaux and Johnson 2013; White, Harvey, and Abu-Rayya 2015); this relates directly to the focus on generalization from my framework.

The framework from Section 2 also suggests other ways to improve the preceding experiments. Thus far, the experiments have only considered measures of political support and not interpersonal perceptions of the outgroup member. While critical to democratic theory and politics, this limits the way these results apply to more general interpersonal and intergroup attitudes. Further, do the results from the in-person encounters in experiments 1 and 2 translate into increasingly common computer-mediated settings?

Experiment 3 was designed to address these issues. Relying on a panel of respondents from a large market research firm, I conducted an online survey experiment in the spring of 2018 with a diverse sample of White American adults. Consistent with both prior studies, this experiment involved an outgroup member who either presented themselves in an easy- or hard-to-understand way. The design of this study used a two-wave approach to analyze the different effects of contact among those who do and do not avoid interactions with outgroup members. The experiment further expands the previous two by measuring a wide set of group-based attitudes to explore the boundaries of contact's social and political consequences.

In this experiment, I find that perceptions of the outgroup member in contact vary in ways expected by the literature on equal status and the ease of communicating. I again fail to find support for $H_{Contact}$ but do not observe the backlash predicted by H_{Threat}. Crucially, these results do not depend on respondents' preexisting willingness to interact with outgroups.

4.3.1 Theory

$H_{Contact}$ and H_{Threat} describe how individuals react to outgroup members once they participate in an interaction. How, though, do these effects vary depending on the context and on individuals' propensities to choose to interact with outgroup members?

Context

In general, different kinds of physical settings influence important psychological concepts like mood and judgments about others (Schwarz and Clore 2003). Building on these ideas, some studies on social outgroups and communications have taken the notion of context seriously: isolated images of outgroup members prompt many of the same threat-based cognitive processes as actual interactions with outgroup members (Richeson et al. 2003), and online forms of intergroup contact seem to produce comparable reactions as in-person studies (Alvídrez et al. 2015; White, Harvey, and Abu-Rayya 2015). Some of the conversational norms observed in face-to-face interaction have also been documented in online environments (Oeberst and Moskaliuk 2016). As such, I consider how the results observed in prior experiments are replicated in a different context – in online settings with videos of outgroup members. This is especially critical in the age of internet communications and new media, when many new forms of online interpersonal interactions are developing rapidly.

Willingness to Interact with Outgroups

Experiment 2 discusses the importance of considering those who do and do not choose to interact with outgroup members but could only consider the attitudes of those who chose to experience contact. As such, it is unclear how those findings apply to individuals who opt out of opportunities for contact.

In this area, existing research presents conflicting expectations. Some research indicates that those who opt out of outgroup experiences should react more negatively to contact. Those who opt out of experiences with outgroup members may have stronger anti-outgroup attitudes and rely more on their stereotypes of outgroups when interacting with outgroup members (Binder et al. 2009; Swart et al. 2011; Christ et al. 2014). These individuals may also be those who have had more negative contact experiences in the past, which can influence how future experiences are interpreted (Barlow et al. 2012; Paolini et al. 2014). Those with especially strong negative attitudes about outgroups may also interpret the contact experience largely in line with their preexisting negative attitudes about that group; this would be consistent with research on confirmation bias, attitude strength, and selective exposure (Brannon, Tagler, and Eagly 2007; Knobloch-Westerwick and Meng 2009; Howe and Krosnick 2017). Accordingly, those who opt out of contact but experience it anyway should react to contact more negatively than others, consistent with research on racial threat more generally (Major, Blodorn, and Blascovich 2016).

Other perspectives, however, suggest different possibilities. Research on moral licensing, for example, suggests that expressing a willingness to engage with outgroup members might lead to *lower* support for outgroups. Those who express a willingness to engage in outgroup contact may feel less constrained by egalitarian social norms later on in expressing their support for outgroups (Blanken, van de Ven, and Zeelenberg 2015). This is because individuals no longer need to defend their self-image as a moral individual after expressing these ostensibly pro-social views. A separate point of view would propose that individuals who are open to engaging with outgroups already have many of these experiences, making an additional encounter relatively ineffective in changing their views and beliefs (this would be a clear example of pretreatment effects; see Druckman and Leeper 2012). Given these possibilities, I examine both sets of respondents for differences without directional, a priori expectations and formulate a research question (RQ1), rather than a more formal hypothesis.

RQ1: Do those who do and do not opt out of contact experiences show support for $H_{Contact}$, H_{Threat}, or neither?

4.3.2 Design

To evaluate these ideas, I conducted an online survey experiment through Bovitz, Inc., a market research firm that maintains a large, high-quality panel of potential respondents. The demographics of the sample are listed in Table 7, along with comparable statistics from the 2016 American National Election Study (ANES), a high-quality probability sample of the population of the United States.[19] While not strictly representative, the Bovitz sample is diverse along many dimensions (ideology, age, income, etc.), which is more critical for experimental research than strict representativeness (Druckman and Kam 2011).

The data were collected in two waves. In the first wave, respondents provided their consent to participate and were presented with a welcome screen. Subjects then completed a set of demographic items, including gender, age, racial and ethnic identity, prior contact with racial groups, political ideology, party

---

[19] The numbers in the table are for individuals who completed waves one and two. The Online Appendix contains a parallel demographic table for the complete set of wave one respondents and a discussion of nonresponse.

Table 7 Experiment 3 sample demographics

	2018 Bovitz sample	*2016 ANES (unweighted)*
Age (median)	44	50
Income (median)	$50,000 to $75,000	$35,000 to $39,999
Education (median)	Some college	Associates degree
Percent Female	47.4%	53%
Percent conservative	40.3%	42%
Percent liberal	31.3%	22%
Political interest (mean)	3.4 out of 5	2.1 out of 4
N	642	4,271

identification, and the extent to which they value benevolence, universalism, achievement, power, equality, civil liberties, self-reliance, and law and order.[20]

After these demographic variables, I measured subjects' tendencies to avoid intergroup contact through a timed word puzzle. Subjects were introduced into a timed word puzzle task that they would later be asked to discuss with a partner. The task is adapted from studies of partisan prejudice (Lelkes and Westwood 2017), and it involves filling in a partially-completed word with a given clue.[21] After completing three such puzzles, subjects were shown their score and informed that they would be randomly assigned to a partner to "discuss what makes someone do well or poorly on the word puzzles and how you felt about your score." Importantly, subjects were told repeatedly that they would speak to their partner via an online chat window.

Subjects were presented with an outrace partner, as described with the graphic in Figure 8. The nonracial characteristics were extensively pretested to avoid artificially encouraging or discouraging conversations with this individual. The consequence of this description is that the potential partner may vary from the subject in several ways *besides* race; however, such differences and confounding are inevitable in actual social experiences. This measure was designed with these dynamics in mind to serve as a more accurate behavioral measure of one's avoidance of outgroup experiences and overcome many of the problems of self-reported racial attitudes and prior contact. Additionally,

---

[20] Each value is measured with a single item (Schwartz 2003; Schwartz et al. 2014), and was selected for its potential to serve as a moderator (see Sagiv and Schwartz 1995; Goren et al. 2016).

[21] Many thanks to Lelkes and Westwood for providing details on their research. In pilot testing, almost no respondents, regardless of their racial attitudes, excluded racial outgroup members in the set-up used by Lelkes and Westwood. The task as described here is the product of repeated pilot testing with the goal to provide a measure of outgroup rejection that accurately captures respondents' group-based preferences.

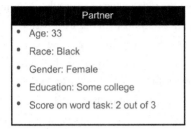

Figure 8 Partner description

interaction with this partner mimicked the form of contact from the prior experiments – a brief conversation with an outgroup stranger on a nonracial topic.

Subjects were then given the choice to either speak with this partner or ask for a new one. They then explained their choice, waited for a few moments, and were then told that they would not be able to complete the word puzzle conversation due to drop out in the study among other participants. They were presented with a few additional items as a substitute for the puzzle, including political interest, feeling thermometers on White and Black people, measures of moral self-image, and items on racial resentment. At this point, wave one was complete.

Subjects were recontacted in about seven days for the second wave, in order to avoid: (1) respondent fatigue and (2) priming effects from the earlier racial items. In wave two, subjects viewed a brief video that served as the form of intergroup contact in the experiment. Subjects saw one of two videos: an easy-to-understand video of a phenotypically Black female and a hard-to-understand video of the same phenotypically Black female. To maximize comparability between all experiments, the individual in the video was one of the administrators from experiment 1. Prior to either video, the speaker was described briefly in this way:

> "As a bit of background, this individual is in her late twenties, lives in an urban area, and identifies as Black and female."

Subjects were encouraged to engage with this video and imagine what it would be like to interact with this person; these elements of the design were modeled after research on how to encourage meaningful imagined forms of intergroup contact (Husnu and Crisp 2011).

The two treatment clips used identical scripts, varying only nonverbal components to make the clips harder or easier to understand. The speaker varied the ease of understanding in the exact ways discussed in the prior experiments (e.g., eye contact, body language, pauses). The video clip treatments were block-randomized by subjects' choice of an outgroup member in wave one; this means that estimates of treatment effects from the video clips are causally identified for both those who did and did not select an outgroup member as a partner. The Online Appendix contains the question wordings, the scripts, and the ways the clips differ.

Following the clips, participants reported their reactions to the outgroup individual, their policy attitudes with reference to several racial groups, their tolerance for different kinds of demonstrations, and a battery of racial- and group-based attitudes. The items in this section included the questions used in the previous experiments: support for government action in education and employment, the criminal justice system, affirmative action in colleges, and demonstrations advocating for Black individuals under a number of conditions. Subjects were then debriefed, and their participation was complete. The complete design is summarized in Figure 9.

As indicated in this description, experiment 3 focused on the outgroup of Black people, in contrast to the emphasis on Latinx individuals in experiment 2. This choice allows experiment 3 to generalize the findings from experiment 1, which focused on interactions between Black and White individuals, and extend experiment 2. Further work should continue to explore the similarities and differences between various types of racial and ethnic contact.

4.3.3 Results

The first element of these analyses explores the measure of outgroup engagement – the choice to reject or accept the outgroup partner in wave one. Only about 9 percent of the sample rejected the outgroup partner, suggesting that most were open to this kind of outgroup contact. Those who chose not to interact with the outgroup partner expressed higher levels of racial resentment ($p=0.01$), higher levels of ethnocentrism ($p\sim0.00$), lower levels of prior contact with racial minorities ($p\sim0.00$), and higher racial identification with their own group

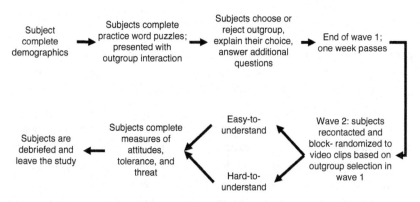

Figure 9 Experiment 3 design

(p~0.00). They also placed less importance on the values of benevolence (p~0.00), universalism (p~0.00), equality (p~0.00), and civil liberties (p~0.00). Finally, they were also more politically conservative (p=0.01). More complex analyses that account for nonracial differences between subjects and the offered partner confirm these results (see Online Appendix for more details). Even holding nonracial differences with the partner constant, the choice to accept the outgroup partner reliably correlates with more positive feelings toward and engagement with Black individuals, lower levels of racial polarization, and reduced ethnocentrism.

The analyses of the video treatments, like those used previously, rely on NPC to test the core hypotheses, $H_{Contact}$ and H_{Threat}. Unlike the preceding experiments, experiment 3 included a wide range of measures about the outgroup individual in the video and Black people generally. I first examine these items. Figure 10 shows the difference between the easy and hard forms of contact along a set of variables about the Black individual. Subjects were asked to explicitly indicate how easy it was to understand the speaker (outgroup member, presented as Eboni), how similar the speaker was to them, and how they perceived her on various dimensions relevant to the theories used here (competence, warmth, etc.). In each condition, subjects also described what they learned from the video clip; these responses were coded for references to race to evaluate if racial boundaries were more salient in one condition or the other.

Figure 10 suggests clear treatment effects (on the overall and individual p-values) and indicates two important things. First, the easy-to-understand conditions prompt more conversational ease and similarity, indicating that these treatments worked as described in earlier sections. Second, the easy

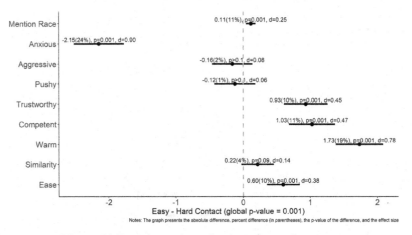

Figure 10 Experiment 3 results, interpersonal measures

outgroup conversations promoted a more positive impression of Eboni – she is rated as warmer, more competent, more trustworthy, and less anxious. In this condition, subjects were also more likely to explicitly mention race in describing what they learned about Eboni. These latter two points, interpersonal positivity and a higher salience of race, indicate some possibility of optimism: positivity toward Eboni does not seem to be a product of failing to recognize relevant racial boundaries, and improved personal impressions can coexist with salient group divisions.

Figure 11 describes these patterns among those who did and did not avoid the outgroup partner in wave one. The ease of communication seems to operate similarly for both groups, irrespective of one's hesitancy about engaging with outrace individuals.

Having established these initial perceptions, I now turn to the main measures of outgroup support. These include support for government action to ensure fairness in criminal justice, government action to ensure equal opportunities in education and employment, support for preferential treatment in college admissions (affirmative action), and support for a demonstration advocating for Black people under different conditions. These are the same measures used in experiments 1 and 2. Figure 12 shows the differences in support for Black people between the easy and hard conditions.

In no case do I find statistically significant differences between these treatment groups on measures of outgroup support. This is true of the individual variables (p-values range from 0.57 to 0.81) and the global NPC p-value listed on the figure.

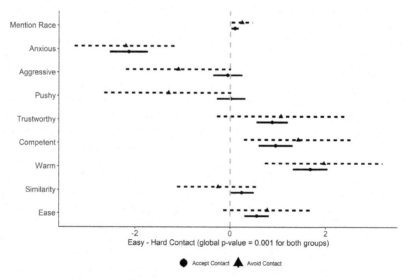

Figure 11 Experiment 3 results by contact acceptance

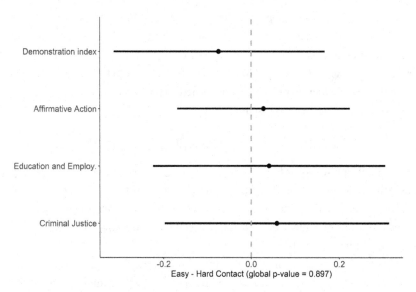

Figure 12 Experiment 3 results, political measures

This is also true for both those who do and do not avoid the outgroup partner on wave one (global p-values above 0.70 in both cases). I also conducted different robustness checks for the analyses presented in the previous tables, including bootstrapped analyses, regressions with interactive terms, and estimates that control for other variables. Equivalency testing, which determines if nonsignificant findings can be equated with an absence of treatment effects (Lakens 2017), further indicate that these treatments do not generate a meaningful change in support for the outgroup in this experience. These analyses all lead to the same conclusion: attitudes toward Black people do not change in response to this form of contact. As such, I again fail to find any support for $H_{Contact}$ but also do not observe the backlash associated with H_{Threat}.

4.3.4 Discussion

Unlike in the previous experiments, I find little support for the idea that people react differently to easy and hard communications with outgroup members. Although easy interactions promote more positive impressions of outgroup *individuals*, this does not lead to changes in support for the group as a whole. This lack of differences is also not contingent on individuals' standing attitudes with regards to race.

These findings have implications for the conclusions from the prior two experiments. Across all three studies, I consistently fail to find support for $H_{Contact}$, the idea that easier, more equal-status interactions with outgroups promote more outgroup support. Given the results in other settings, this suggests that there may be no clear benefit to structuring contact to promote understanding between groups, despite the intuitive appeal of such efforts. In contrast, I fail to replicate the backlash predicted by H_{Threat}, indicating a need to consider why this would occur in experiments 1 and 2 but not here (a point to which I turn in the next experiment and the general discussion).

4.4 Experiment 4: Survey Experiment, MTurk Version

As a final application of my framework, I conducted an additional survey experiment to replicate the findings from experiment 3 and explore how explicit hostility from the outgroup member changes the political consequences of easy and hard forms of contact. This survey was conducted on Amazon's Mechanical Turk in the winter of 2019.

Ultimately, this experiment replicates many of the findings from the prior experiments. The ease of communication treatments shift impressions of the outgroup member, as theorized. Once again, I fail to observe results consistent with $H_{Contact}$. I observe some mixed evidence for H_{Threat}, although the results are more muted than in experiments 1 and 2. Independently encouraging feelings of threat from the outgroup member do not change the results observed in the prior experiments.

4.4.1 Theory

Like the other experiments, the key hypotheses in experiment 4 involve comparisons between easy and hard forms of intergroup contact to evaluate both $H_{Contact}$ and H_{Threat}. As such, I rely on the same theoretical orientation from the prior studies. In addition, I consider here how explicit hostility on the part of the outgroup member does or does not change the consequences of easy-to-understand forms of contact.

Like the prior experiments, experiment 3 found no support for $H_{Contact}$, raising questions about the role of equal status as a method to improve contact's ability to increase support for outgroups. On the other hand, experiment 3 did not find evidence in favor of H_{Threat}. This may have been from decreased feelings of threat in the online format: in computer-mediated settings, social and psychological distance between the respondent and outgroup members is likely higher. This, in turn, should be associated with decreased feelings of threat due simply to the medium. Perceptions of threat and distance are intimately linked; specifically, threatening objects are perceived of as closer and closer objects are thought to be more threatening (e.g., Loewenstein et al. 2001; Harber, Yeung, and Iacovelli 2011; Xiao and Van Bavel 2012).

One way of evaluating this proposition is to more directly increase the threatening nature of the outgroup member. If these ideas about psychological distance are correct, respondents in an online environment may not be attentive to the relatively subtle group threat created by the equal-status treatments. This could be caused by a number of factors; for example, the outgroup member is not physically present, and people's attention may be drawn elsewhere. However, when these equal-status cues are paired with more direct group threats, the status-based implications of outgroups' nonverbal behavior may be accentuated and generate more resentment and threat. Alternative literatures on racial threats and attitudes, however, propose that direct threats may not have these consequences. Like some kinds of racial messages, it may be that explicit threats to White Americans' status engage White people's ideas about racial egalitarianism and broader racial norms (Mendelberg 2001; Reny, Valenzuela, and Collingwood 2019; cf., Valentino, Neuner, and Vandenbroek 2018). This would further undermine, not enhance, the consequences of the ease-of-communication treatments. Given these different expectations, I again consider this as a research question, summarized as RQ2.

RQ2: Are ease-of-communication status threats made more potent by direct racial hostility?

4.4.2 Design

Experiment 4 had a similar structure to experiment 3, with a few modifications to evaluate RQ2. The experiment utilized a single wave of responses collected through Amazon's Mechanical Turk (MTurk). This platform has been extensively evaluated by political scientists; while not representative of the American population, MTurk provides a low-cost, rapid data collection outlet well suited to the causally-oriented work of experiments (Berinsky, Huber, and Lenz 2012; Mullinix et al. 2015; Coppock 2018).

White American individuals on MTurk were invited to participate in the experiment and first completed a few demographic items. Notably, the word-puzzle task was omitted due to concerns about space and how credible the word-puzzle partner task would be to respondents on MTurk. The failure to find heterogeneous treatment effects based on outgroup avoidance also supports this omission choice. Following the demographic items, subjects viewed a brief description of the same outrace individual from experiment 3, watched the same videos of this individual from experiment 3, completed similar items about perceptions of her, and answered questions about outgroup support drawn from experiments 1 and 2. Subjects were then debriefed, and their participation was complete.

This experiment involved two levels of treatments to consider $H_{Contact}$, H_{Threat}, and RQ2 simultaneously. The first involved how Eboni was described prior to the video clip. For all subjects, Eboni was described as a blogger, and a screenshot of one of her blog posts was shown to subjects. In the nonthreatening condition, this post discussed why Eboni always writes down what she thinks. This blog post was created to send no additional information about Eboni and provide a comparable baseline for the threatening condition. In the threatening condition, subjects were shown a blog post about how Eboni thinks White people are harming America. This treatment was drafted such that it critiqued White Americans broadly (not, for example, by political affiliation or region) and sent a message about racial hostility to subjects. These treatments varied only in their titles and subtitles to maintain as much comparability as possible across the treatment conditions. Figures 13 and 14 present these treatments.

https://thefrequentblogger.com

Why I blog as often and much as I can
No matter how I am or am not feeling

This is something that has been on my mind for quite some time. I've finally decided to write it into a blog post. I know that many of you may disagree. But that's exactly why I decided to write about it – I think my voice and the voice of people like me ought to be heard.

I first started thinking about this years ago when I was finishing high school.

Figure 13 Nonthreatening description

https://thefrequentblogger.com

Why white people are ruining America
No matter what they say or where they're from

This is something that has been on my mind for quite some time. I've finally decided to write it into a blog post. I know that many of you may disagree. But that's exactly why I decided to write about it – I think my voice and the voice of people like me ought to be heard.

I first started thinking about this years ago when I was finishing high school.

Figure 14 Threatening description

The second level of treatments were the same easy and hard conversational components used in experiments 1, 2, and 3. The videos used here were the same clips as in experiment 3. The threat and contact treatments were fully crossed, creating four treatment conditions. Table 8 shows these treatments and the number of subjects in each cell. The key comparisons involve the easy and hard forms of contact and differences between these comparisons under threatening and nonthreatening conditions. The Online Appendix contains the full question wording and additional details for this experiment.

4.4.3 Results

Table 9 presents the demographic characteristics of the MTurk sample, shown alongside the sample from experiment 3 for comparison. While not representative, the MTurk sample shows a fair amount of diversity, especially as compared to traditional convenience samples.

To evaluate $H_{Contact}$, H_{Threat}, and RQ2, I again rely on NPC analyses. Figure 15 shows that subjects perceive the easy-to-understand individual as more competent, warmer, more similar to themselves, and easier to understand than in the hard-to-understand clip. Additionally, subjects in the easy-to-understand condition are again more likely to mention race in open-ended items. These patterns are identical in their direction and substance to the ones presented from experiment 3 in Figure 11. The patterns in Figure 15 do not change if I consider only those

Table 8 Experiment 4 design

	Nonthreatening	Threatening
Easy contact	C1: 165	C3: 160
Hard contact	C2: 139	C4: 138

Table 9 Experiment 4 sample demographics

	2019 MTurk sample	*2018 Bovitz sample*
Age (median)	29	44
Income (median)	$35,000 to $50,000	$50,000 to $75,000
Education (median)	4-year college degree	Some college
Percent Female	65%	47.4%
Percent conservative	30.8%	40.3%
Percent liberal	54.6%	31.3%
N	602	642

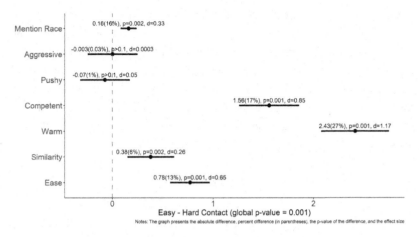

Figure 15 Experiment 4, interpersonal measures

conditions with the racially hostile or nonthreatening blog post from Eboni, suggesting that these reactions do not depend on increased racial threat from the outgroup member. By and large, easy forms of intergroup contact promote more equal-status impressions of outgroup individuals.

Figure 16 presents the results of the NPC analyses on the measures of political support for Black people. The findings here bear some similarities to both experiments 2 and 3 from this section. In general, and as indicated by the global NPC p-value, there seems to be no difference in political support depending on the type of contact people experience. Equal-status contact, once again, does not promote increased outgroup support more than different forms of contact. On one measure of support for political action (when the demonstration blocks traffic), the easy form of contact may again *lower* political support; the direction of the effects for all the demonstration items also suggests this possibility. Equivalency tests support the conclusions presented in Figure 16 – there is a very low probability of meaningful treatment effects for all of the outcomes except attitudes about the demonstration blocking traffic and the demonstration clashing with police. As in Figure 15, these patterns do not change if I consider only those who did or did not see the threatening version of the outgroup member.

4.4.4 Discussion

Experiment 4 presents both confirmations and surprises. In general, reactions to the outgroup individual seem the same as in experiment 3. The measures of political support are similar to the failure to support $H_{Contact}$ in all of the prior studies. There is also some suggestive evidence of a backlash, as in experiment

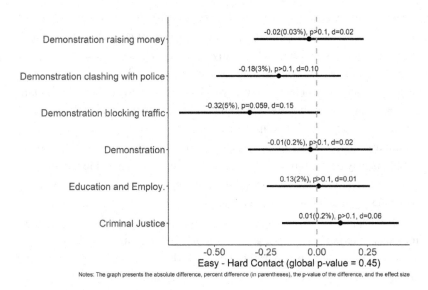

Figure 16 Experiment 4, political measures

2. Interestingly, explicitly threatening and hostile messages from the outgroup member do not shift reactions to contact – there is no evidence that the threat treatments change how people react to easy- and hard-to-understand forms of interracial contact. This may be due to the fact that the theories behind H_{Threat} work through a process of status and identity threat, whereas the threat-based treatments in this experiment seem to be more about general antipathy and hostility. Accordingly, more work needs to be done in this area to distinguish between different kinds of threats from outgroups and how different modes of interaction accentuate or attenuate those threats.

4.5 General Discussion

Across all three earlier experiments and in the previous section, I find no support for $H_{Contact}$. More equal-status contact, as created by the ease of communication, never promoted more support for outgroups than other types of contact. This occurred no matter when, where, or with whom the experiments were conducted. In some circumstances, people responded to easier-to-understand forms of contact with *lower* amounts of political support for outgroups. Connecting the ease of communication to status perceptions presents a challenge to the proposition in contact theory that equal-status contact can improve relationships between groups – none of the experiments discussed here provide evidence supporting the idea that equal status can promote more positive reactions to intergroup contact.

Other conclusions from these studies point to ways that these patterns can be magnified. Reactions to different kinds of contact have the potential to spill over to related groups that are not directly involved in the contact experience. Negative political reactions to contact, then, may have broad implications for closely associated groups in American society (e.g., Latinx people and immigrants, Republicans and Evangelicals). When presented with the choice to engage in or refuse intergroup contact, people seem more likely to interact with individuals who are more similar to them; however, these same outgroup members may go on to prompt a sense of intergroup threat and lower levels of political support. At the very least, these findings suggest that outgroup members who promote more intergroup engagement are not more likely to increase political support for their group. Attempts to encourage intergroup experiences may therefore fail to improve group relationships and might, in some circumstances, produce unexpected backlashes even when they increase the amount of contact between groups.

None of these conclusions would be apparent without applying the framework from Section 2. This approach to contact research dramatically expands the knowledge that contact researchers can produce, a point to which I now turn.

5 Conclusion

Groups are central to democratic society. They influence individual-level behavior (Kinder and Kam 2009; Kinder and Kalmoe 2017), political institutions (Weir 1992; Soss, Fording, and Schram 2011; Hamilton, Madison, and Jay 2014), and the nature of democracy (Dahl 1989; Achen and Bartels 2016). As various democratic theorists note, the relationships between social groups can buttress or undermine democratic government (Sullivan, Piereson, and Marcus 1982; Dahl 1989; Taylor 1994). For many, then, the key question is how to encourage harmonious relationships and recognition between groups.

What forms of intergroup contact promote the cross-group political support and tolerance central to many versions of democracy? This Element proposed a four-part framework for answering this question through experiments. The empirical core of this Element then described four experiments designed with these recommendations in mind. These studies therefore both contribute to the study of contact and illustrate the proposed scaffolding for conducting research in this area.

Several conclusions emerge from these experiments. First, and most strikingly, more equal status, easy-to-understand interactions with outgroup members never increased political support for those groups. I find no evidence for the proposition that addressing difficulties in communicating promotes support for policies and actions in favor of racial and ethnic outgroups. This is true across samples, formats, and time. In multiple circumstances – the lab experiment, the field study, and the online MTurk survey – easy-to-understand interactions can provoke a backlash in a way consistent with theories about racial threat. Despite the intuitive appeal of reducing communication barriers between groups, simple efforts to promote easier interactions are unlikely to encourage more support for outgroups.

On this point, I find a more threat-based reaction to equal-status contact in experiments 1 and 2 than in experiments 3 and 4. One of the main differences in these two sets of studies is the mode through which contact is administered – either in person or through the internet. This raises questions about the ways different contexts amplify group and status-based threats. Most of the proposed conditions of contact are intended to reduce the threat and anxiety created by contact; different media used for communicating, then, may also reduce group-based threats. More needs to be done to discover what platforms might promote more positivity toward outgroups, as the experiments here only succeeded in making different forms of contact more comparable. Additional studies should also directly compare this type of mode effect with the conditions proposed by Allport, an issue studies of contact have not yet considered.

Two of the four experiments also found that easier forms of interactions across groups promote more positive assessments of specific outgroup members. This finding, in combination with the political support measures, suggests that there may be an especially high hurdle in promoting *political* support for outgroups rather than merely improved feelings toward particular individuals. Social scientists have long noted a principle-policy gap in many individuals' political views (Jackman 1978; 1996; Rabinowitz et al. 2009; Tuch and Hughes 2011); the findings discussed in the previous sections support this perspective. Those interested in the potential of intergroup contact for democracy, then, should consider how to overcome this gap and go beyond approaches focusing on improving interpersonal perceptions and general attitudes toward groups.

These findings are not the artifact of one particular study. The four experiments stretch across four years (2016, 2017, 2018, and 2019). They utilize different samples in different contexts: a student sample in a lab, a nonstudent adult sample in a realistic setting, an online experiment with a nationally diverse adult sample, and an online convenience sample. In addition, the experiments explore two different racial and ethnic forms of contact: interactions between Black and White individuals and between Latinx and non-Latinx people. There are other ways to improve the generalizability of these experiments, but this set of studies provides evidence that goes beyond any one context or group within the American public.

5.1 Implications for the Study of Contact

These experiments have implications for the study of intergroup contact in political science and the social sciences more broadly. At a general level, these experiments raise questions about the role of equal status in intergroup contact – the data discussed in the previous sections provides no evidence that increased status perceptions of outgroups boost outgroup support. In some circumstances, it even does the opposite.

These findings also illustrate the importance of focusing on the framework from Section 2: creating specific forms of intergroup contact, harmonizing multiple relevant social science theories, considering a range of outcomes, and designing experiments to intentionally boost generalizability. Without these components, even the causal inferences from experiments can help very little in determining how different kinds of contact influence democratic society.

Every experiment in this Element intentionally created contact experiences that differed only in the ease of understanding, and therefore the perceived status, of the outgroup member. As a result, these experiments speak directly to the consequences of contact under different conditions – a central question for researchers since contact theory was first developed (e.g., Allport 1954; Blalock 1967). By intentionally creating and varying contact along specific, intentional dimensions, researchers can study contact in a way that builds on the weaknesses of current studies in this area (e.g., Paluck, Green, and Green 2018) and makes the strongest causal inferences possible about the conditions that promote more positive reactions to outgroups.

Each design also incorporated various theories from across the social sciences. The main hypotheses tested across the experiments ($H_{Contact}$ and H_{Threat}) involved theories about social identity, contact, and intergroup threat. The focus on conversational difficulty came from theories on processing fluency and conversational norms. Perspectives on interviewer effects, survey response, moral licensing, and more provide insight into the larger dynamics at work in intergroup contact. Integrating these ideas helps to understand contact in a richer way and consider the role of many components of intergroup experiences.

Considering a range of outcomes is also critical for work on contact and democracy. For the experiments in this Element, focusing only on political support would have overlooked the way interpersonal impressions change in response to conversational difficulty. Given the scope of most political science research, it is essential to consider individual impressions, group attitudes, and various measures of political support. This is where political science is uniquely poised to supplement more general psychological work – political scientists' emphasis on political and policy outcomes allows them to consider how psychological work applies not just to interpersonal impressions but also to more abstract and complex political views.

Finally, an intentional focus on generalizability is key for contact experiments. Contact research has moved past the mere demonstration of effects to more complex and nuanced discussions. Further, many have raised concerns about differences in reactions to contact across social groups and settings; as a consequence, researchers should intentionally implement ways to evaluate the boundaries of their conclusions. Even when this leads to unexpected findings, such surprises promote more accurate and limited interpretations of experimental findings and prompt additional theoretical development. Each of the experiments in this Element is restricted in its generalizability; the lab experiment, for example, uses only university students in an artificial lab setting. However, combined, these experiments make a much more robust and persuasive case about the political consequences of different forms of contact than any single experiment.

Researchers are not obligated to follow each of these recommendations; indeed, very little could compel them to do so. However, experimentation as a method, despite its causal strengths, is not a panacea to the issues facing contact research. A specific approach to experiments, though, could dramatically improve this work and its application to the problems facing democratic society in the United States. This area of the social sciences (and many others) requires thorough, intentional, and repeated experiments to overcome the uncertainties, inconsistencies, and gaps in the existing literature.

5.2 Implications for Intergroup Contact and Democracy

Beyond the framework from Section 2 and discussions of experimentation, these results have substantive implications about the role of intergroup contact in democracy. Groups are a perpetual part of politics, and group divisions are receiving increasing attention in the current political moment. While sometimes beneficial in terms of mobilization and engagement, such divisions can increase interpersonal conflict, decrease political tolerance, and encourage group-based biases (e.g., Chanley 1994; J. R. Chambers, Baron, and Inman 2006; Greenwald and Pettigrew 2014). These group-based behaviors have implications for democratic society as they prevent the inclusion, recognition, and tolerance of various kinds of groups, especially those with little social or political power and influence.

Intergroup contact has an intuitive appeal as a resolution to these problems. Given continuing segregation in the geographic, social, and economic spaces Americans inhabit, the American public is far from achieving the ideal of regular, sustained encounters across group boundaries. Intuitively and according to certain theories, contact seems like a straightforward, commonsense solution to these social and physical boundaries between people.

However, from its inception, contact theorists have cautioned that contact is not a guaranteed path to group-based harmony. Foundational works in contact explored key conditions under which contact would lead to less prejudice and group-based threats (Allport 1954; Pettigrew 1998). And although much of current research takes a more expansive view (Pettigrew and Tropp 2011), the core question remains – what kinds of intergroup experiences can improve group relationships, rather than making them worse?

The experiments presented in this Element suggest serious pitfalls in relying on improvements in communications to promote positive forms of contact. Easier communications offer no improvement over more difficult encounters; in fact, they can undermine, rather than bolster, outgroup support. Despite its simplicity and ability to improve interpersonal perceptions, intergroup contact based on ease of communications falls short of generating the reactions desired by contact and democratic theorists.

The conclusions from Sections 3 and 4 also present an important tension: the outgroup members most likely to encourage intergroup interactions may go on to depress support for their group. This places a normatively problematic burden on minority groups to present themselves initially in engaging, confident ways while still appearing deferential as contact proceeds. In the end, these findings suggest the need for careful research on group-focused interventions – appealing, intuitive ideas can backfire in unintended ways. Further, these experiments highlight the difficulty in increasing outgroup support; the most "positive" reaction from these experiments was a failure to change attitudes, a rather low bar.

Other group experiences and mindsets may hold more promise. Some researchers studying intergroup relationships suggest that with time, repeated experiences with outgroups can mute negative reactions to initial forms of intergroup contact (Toosi et al. 2012; Enos 2014; MacInnis and Page-Gould 2015). However, numerous questions remain about how this process unfolds, the conditions under which repeated contact softens initial, negative reactions, and ways to maintain such repeated contact. As such, a great deal of careful experimental and theoretical work is needed before repeated, sustained contact can be reliably connected to increased political support for outgroups.

Different perspectives suggest other possibilities. An emphasis on different kinds of blame attribution, for example, may encourage individuals to help and support groups in need (Reisenzein 1986; Schmidt and Weiner 1988). Shifting the kinds of stereotypes individuals bring to mind about various groups could also reduce group-based polarization (Rothschild et al. 2019). Considering how to promote social change alongside improved interpersonal impressions is one key need in this area of study (Dixon et al. 2010; Saguy and Chernyak-Hai 2012). Applying these insights in a way that improves the attitudes of many kinds of individuals – not just majority group members – is also of great importance. Contact that explicitly discusses and addresses group-based threat and status expectations might help to undo the backlash discovered here. While these suggestions are still untested, it is the kind of discussion that social scientists should have when considering the role of contact in democratic politics. Only through careful empirical investigation and subsequent rethinking can interested researchers effectively uncover ways to promote the kinds of group-based tolerance and support that democracy sorely needs.

References

Abrajano, Marisa, and Zoltan L. Hajnal. 2015. *White Backlash: Immigration, Race, and American Politics*. Princeton: Princeton University Press.

Achen, Christopher H., and Larry M. Bartels. 2016. *Democracy for Realists: Why Elections Do Not Produce Responsive Government*. Princeton: Princeton University Press.

Allport, Gordon W. 1954. *The Nature of Prejudice*. Reading, MA: Addison-Wesley.

Alter, Adam L., and Daniel M. Oppenheimer. 2009. "Uniting the Tribes of Fluency to Form a Metacognitive Nation." *Personality and Social Psychology Review* 13 (3): 219–235.

Alvídrez, Salvador, Valeriano Piñeiro-Naval, María Marcos-Ramos, and José Luis Rojas-Solís. 2015. "Intergroup Contact in Computer-Mediated Communication: The Interplay of a Stereotype-Disconfirming Behavior and a Lasting Group Identity on Reducing Prejudiced Perceptions." *Computers in Human Behavior* 52 (November): 533–540.

Arceneaux, Kevin, and Martin Johnson. 2013. *Changing Minds or Changing Channels? Partisan News in an Age of Choice*. Chicago: University of Chicago Press.

Bachrach, Peter, and Morton S. Baratz. 1962. "Two Faces of Power." *The American Political Science Review* 56 (4): 947–952.

Bagci, Sabahat C., and Abbas Turnuklu. 2019. "Intended, Unintended, and Unknown Consequences of Contact: The Role of Positive–Negative Contact on Outgroup Attitudes, Collective Action Tendencies, and Psychological Well-Being." *Social Psychology* 50 (1): 7–23.

Balliet, Daniel, Junhui Wu, and Carsten K. W. De Dreu. 2014. "Ingroup Favoritism in Cooperation: A Meta-Analysis." *Psychological Bulletin* 140 (6): 1556–1581.

Barber, Benjamin R. 1984. *Strong Democracy: Participatory Politics for a New Age*. Berkeley: University of California Press.

Barlow, Fiona Kate, Stefania Paolini, Anne Pedersen, Matthew J. Hornsey, Helena R. M. Radke, Jake Harwood, Mark Rubin, and Chris G. Sibley. 2012. "The Contact Caveat Negative Contact Predicts Increased Prejudice More Than Positive Contact Predicts Reduced Prejudice." *Personality and Social Psychology Bulletin* 38 (12): 1629–1643.

Barth, Jay, L. Marvin Overby, and Scott H. Huffmon. 2009. "Community Context, Personal Contact, and Support for an Anti-Gay Rights Referendum." *Political Research Quarterly* 62 (2): 355–365.

Barth, Jay, and Janine Parry. 2009. "2 > 1 + 1? The Impact of Contact with Gay and Lesbian Couples on Attitudes about Gays/Lesbians and Gay-Related Policies." *Politics & Policy* 37 (1): 31–50.

Berinsky, Adam J., Gregory A. Huber, and Gabriel S. Lenz. 2012. "Evaluating Online Labor Markets for Experimental Research: Amazon.com's Mechanical Turk." *Political Analysis* 20 (3): 351–368.

Berinsky, Adam J., and Donald R. Kinder. 2006. "Making Sense of Issues Through Media Frames: Understanding the Kosovo Crisis." *The Journal of Politics* 68 (3): 640–656.

Berkowitz, Leonard, and Edward Donnerstein. 1982. "External Validity Is More than Skin Deep: Some Answers to Criticisms of Laboratory Experiments." *American Psychologist* 37 (3): 245–257.

Bettencourt, B., Kelly Charlton, Nancy Dorr, and Deborah L. Hume. 2001. "Status Differences and In-Group Bias: A Meta-Analytic Examination of the Effects of Status Stability, Status Legitimacy, and Group Permeability." *Psychological Bulletin* 127 (4): 520–542.

Binder, Jens, Hanna Zagefka, Rupert Brown, Friedrich Funke, Thomas Kessler, Amelie Mummendey, Annemie Maquil, Stephanie Demoulin, and Jacques-Philippe Leyens. 2009. "Does Contact Reduce Prejudice or Does Prejudice Reduce Contact? A Longitudinal Test of the Contact Hypothesis among Majority and Minority Groups in Three European Countries." *Journal of Personality and Social Psychology* 96 (4): 843–856.

Bishoff, Kendra, and Sean F. Reardon. 2014. "Residential Segregation by Income, 1970–2009." In *The Lost Decade? Social Change in the U.S. after 2000*, edited by John R. Logan, 208–234. New York: Russell Sage Foundation.

Blalock, Hubert M. 1967. *Toward a Theory of Minority-Group Relations*. New York: Wiley.

Blanken, Irene, Niels van de Ven, and Marcel Zeelenberg. 2015. "A Meta-Analytic Review of Moral Licensing." *Personality and Social Psychology Bulletin* 41 (4): 540–558.

Blinder, Scott, Robert Ford, and Elisabeth Ivarsflaten. 2013. "The Better Angels of Our Nature: How the Antiprejudice Norm Affects Policy and Party Preferences in Great Britain and Germany." *American Journal of Political Science* 57 (4): 841–857.

Blumer, Herbert. 1958. "Race Prejudice as a Sense of Group Position." *The Pacific Sociological Review* 1 (1): 3–7.

Bobo, Lawrence D. 2000. "Race and Beliefs about Affirmative Action: Assessing the Effects of Interests, Group Threat, Ideology, and Racism."

In *Racialized Politics: The Debate about Racism in America*, edited by David O. Sears, Lawrence Bobo, and Jim Sidanius, 137–164. Chicago: University of Chicago Press.

Bobo, Lawrence D., and Vincent L. Hutchings. 1996. "Perceptions of Racial Group Competition: Extending Blumer's Theory of Group Position to a Multiracial Social Context." *American Sociological Review* 61: 951–972.

Bodenhausen, Galen V., Sonia K. Kang, and Destiny Peery. 2012. "Social Categorization and the Perception of Social Groups." In *Sage Handbook of Social Cognition*, edited by Susan T. Fiske and C. Neil Macrae, 311–329. Los Angeles: Sage.

Bracic, Ana, Mackenzie Israel-Trummel, and Allyson F. Shortle. 2019. "Is Sexism for White People? Gender Stereotypes, Race, and the 2016 Presidential Election." *Political Behavior* 41 (2): 281–307.

Brannon, Laura A., Michael J. Tagler, and Alice H. Eagly. 2007. "The Moderating Role of Attitude Strength in Selective Exposure to Information." *Journal of Experimental Social Psychology* 43 (4): 611–617.

Brewer, Marilynn B. 1999. "The Psychology of Prejudice: Ingroup Love and Outgroup Hate?" *Journal of Social Issues* 55 (3): 429–444.

Broockman, David, and Joshua Kalla. 2016. "Durably Reducing Transphobia: A Field Experiment on Door-to-Door Canvassing." *Science* 352 (6282): 220–224.

Brown, Kendrick T., Tony N. Brown, James S. Jackson, Robert M. Sellers, and Warde J. Manuel. 2003. "Teammates On and Off the Field? Contact With Black Teammates and the Racial Attitudes of White Student Athletes." *Journal of Applied Social Psychology* 33 (7): 1379–1403.

Cakal, Huseyin, Miles Hewstone, Gerhard Schwär, and Anthony Heath. 2011. "An Investigation of the Social Identity Model of Collective Action and the 'Sedative' Effect of Intergroup Contact among Black and White Students in South Africa." *British Journal of Social Psychology* 50 (4): 606–627.

Caughey, Devin, Allan Dafoe, and Jason Seawright. 2017. "Nonparametric Combination (NPC): A Framework for Testing Elaborate Theories." *The Journal of Politics* 79 (2): 688–701.

Chambers, John R., Robert S. Baron, and Mary L. Inman. 2006. "Misperceptions in Intergroup Conflict: Disagreeing About What We Disagree About." *Psychological Science* 17 (1): 38–45.

Chambers, Simone. 2003. "Deliberative Democratic Theory." *Annual Review of Political Science* 6 (1): 307–326.

Chanley, Virginia. 1994. "Commitment to Political Tolerance: Situational and Activity-Based Differences." *Political Behavior* 16 (3): 343–363.

Christ, Oliver, Katharina Schmid, Simon Lolliot, Hermann Swart, Dietlind Stolle, Nicole Tausch, Ananthi Al Ramiah, Ulrich Wagner, Steven Vertovec, and Miles Hewstone. 2014. "Contextual Effect of Positive Intergroup Contact on Outgroup Prejudice." *Proceedings of the National Academy of Sciences* 111 (11): 3996–4000.

Cohen, Elizabeth G., Marlaine E. Lockheed, and Mark R. Lohman. 1976. "The Center for Interracial Cooperation: A Field Experiment." *Sociology of Education* 49 (1): 47–58.

Cohen, Elizabeth G., and Rachel A. Lotan. 1995. "Producing Equal-Status Interaction in the Heterogeneous Classroom." *American Educational Research Journal* 32 (1): 99–120.

Cohen, Elizabeth G., and Susan S. Roper. 1972. "Modification of Interracial Interaction Disability: An Application of Status Characteristic Theory." *American Sociological Review* 37 (6): 643–657.

Coppock, Alexander. 2018. "Generalizing from Survey Experiments Conducted on Mechanical Turk: A Replication Approach." *Political Science Research and Methods* 7 (3): 613–628.

Craig, Maureen A., and Jennifer A. Richeson. 2014a. "On the Precipice of a 'Majority-Minority' America: Perceived Status Threat from the Racial Demographic Shift Affects White Americans' Political Ideology." *Psychological Science* 25 (6): 1189–1197.

2014b. "More Diverse Yet Less Tolerant? How the Increasingly Diverse Racial Landscape Affects White Americans' Racial Attitudes." *Personality and Social Psychology Bulletin* 40 (6): 750–761.

Cuddy, Amy J. C., Susan T. Fiske, and Peter Glick. 2008. "Warmth and Competence as Universal Dimensions of Social Perception: The Stereotype Content Model and the BIAS Map." In *Advances in Experimental Social Psychology, Vol. 40*, edited by Mark P. Zanna, 61–149. San Diego: Elsevier.

Dahl, Robert A. 1989. *Democracy and Its Critics*. New Haven: Yale University Press.

Danbold, Felix, and Yuen J. Huo. 2015. "No Longer 'All-American'? Whites' Defensive Reactions to Their Numerical Decline." *Social Psychological and Personality Science* 6 (2): 210–218.

Danyluck, Chad, and Elizabeth Page-Gould. 2018. "Intergroup Dissimilarity Predicts Physiological Synchrony and Affiliation in Intergroup Interaction." *Journal of Experimental Social Psychology* 74 (January): 111–120.

Dawson, Michael C. 1995. *Behind the Mule: Race and Class in African-American Politics*. Princeton: Princeton University Press.

Deutsch, Morton, and Mary Evans Collins. 1951. *Interracial Housing: A Psychological Evaluation of a Social Experiment*. Minneapolis: University of Minnesota Press.

Devine, Patricia G. 1989. "Stereotypes and Prejudice: Their Automatic and Controlled Components." *Journal of Personality and Social Psychology* 56 (1): 5–18.

DiPrete, Thomas A., Andrew Gelman, Tyler McCormick, Julien Teitler, and Tian Zheng. 2011. "Segregation in Social Networks Based on Acquaintanceship and Trust." *American Journal of Sociology* 116 (4): 1234–1283.

Dixon, John, Kevin Durrheim, and Colin Tredoux. 2005. "Beyond the Optimal Contact Strategy: A Reality Check for the Contact Hypothesis." *American Psychologist* 60 (7): 697–711.

Dixon, John, Linda R. Tropp, Kevin Durrheim, and Colin Tredoux. 2010. "'Let Them Eat Harmony' Prejudice-Reduction Strategies and Attitudes of Historically Disadvantaged Groups." *Current Directions in Psychological Science* 19 (2): 76–80.

Druckman, James N., and Cindy D. Kam. 2011. "Students as Experimental Participants: A Defense of the 'Narrow Data Base.'" In *Cambridge Handbook of Experimental Political Science*, edited by James N. Druckman, Donald P Green, James H. Kuklinski, and Arthur Lupia, 41–57. New York: Cambridge University Press.

Druckman, James N., and Thomas J. Leeper. 2012. "Learning More from Political Communication Experiments: Pretreatment and Its Effects." *American Journal of Political Science* 56 (4): 875–896.

Durrant, Gabriele B., Robert M. Groves, Laura Staetsky, and Fiona Steele. 2010. "Effects of Interviewer Attitudes and Behaviors on Refusal in Household Surveys." *Public Opinion Quarterly* 74 (1): 1–36.

Ellemers, Naomi, Bertjan Doosje, Ad Van Knippenberg, and Henk Wilke. 1992. "Status Protection in High Status Minority Groups." *European Journal of Social Psychology* 22 (2): 123–140.

Eller, Anja, and Dominic Abrams. 2004. "Come Together: Longitudinal Comparisons of Pettigrew's Reformulated Intergroup Contact Model and the Common Ingroup Identity Model in Anglo-French and Mexican-American Contexts." *European Journal of Social Psychology* 34 (3): 229–256.

Ellison, Christopher G., Heeju Shin, and David L. Leal. 2011. "The Contact Hypothesis and Attitudes Toward Latinos in the United States." *Social Science Quarterly* 92 (4): 938–958.

Emery, Nathan J. 2000. "The Eyes Have It: The Neuroethology, Function and Evolution of Social Gaze." *Neuroscience & Biobehavioral Reviews* 24 (6): 581–604.

Enos, Ryan D. 2014. "Causal Effect of Intergroup Contact on Exclusionary Attitudes." *Proceedings of the National Academy of Sciences* 111 (10): 3699–3704.

2016. "What the Demolition of Public Housing Teaches Us about the Impact of Racial Threat on Political Behavior." *American Journal of Political Science* 60 (1): 123–142.

Enos, Ryan D., and Christopher Celaya. 2018. "The Effect of Segregation on Intergroup Relations." *Journal of Experimental Political Science* 5 (1): 26–38.

Finseraas, Henning, and Andreas Kotsadam. 2017. "Does Personal Contact with Ethnic Minorities Affect Anti-Immigrant Sentiments? Evidence from a Field Experiment." *European Journal of Political Research* 56 (March): 703–722.

Fiske, Susan T. 2015. "Intergroup Biases: A Focus on Stereotype Content." *Current Opinion in Behavioral Sciences* 3 (June): 45–50.

Fiske, Susan T., Amy J. C. Cuddy, Peter Glick, and Jun Xu. 2002. "A Model of (Often Mixed) Stereotype Content: Competence and Warmth Respectively Follow from Perceived Status and Competition." *Journal of Personality and Social Psychology* 82 (6): 878–902.

Gaertner, Samuel L., Jeffrey A. Mann, John F. Dovidio, Audrey J. Murrell, and Marina Pomare. 1990. "How Does Cooperation Reduce Intergroup Bias?" *Journal of Personality and Social Psychology* 59 (4): 692–704.

Gaines, Brian J., and James H. Kuklinski. 2011. "Experimental Estimation of Heterogeneous Treatment Effects Related to Self-Selection." *American Journal of Political Science* 55 (3): 724–736.

Gibson, James L. 2006. "Enigmas of Intolerance: Fifty Years after Stouffer's Communism, Conformity, and Civil Liberties." *Perspectives on Politics* 4 (1): 21–34.

2013. "Measuring Political Tolerance and General Support for Pro–Civil Liberties Policies Notes, Evidence, and Cautions." *Public Opinion Quarterly* 77 (S1): 45–68.

Gilens, Martin. 2000. *Why Americans Hate Welfare: Race, Media, and the Politics of Antipoverty Policy*. Chicago: University of Chicago Press.

Glasford, Demis E., and Justine Calcagno. 2012. "The Conflict of Harmony: Intergroup Contact, Commonality and Political Solidarity between Minority Groups." *Journal of Experimental Social Psychology* 48 (1): 323–328.

Gluszek, Agata, and John F. Dovidio. 2010. "The Way They Speak: A Social Psychological Perspective on the Stigma of Nonnative Accents in Communication." *Personality and Social Psychology Review* 14 (2): 214–237.

Goren, Paul, Harald Schoen, Jason Reifler, Thomas Scotto, and William Chittick. 2016. "A Unified Theory of Value-Based Reasoning and U.S. Public Opinion." *Political Behavior* 38 (4): 977–997.

Greenwald, Anthony G., and Thomas F. Pettigrew. 2014. "With Malice toward None and Charity for Some: Ingroup Favoritism Enables Discrimination." *American Psychologist* 69 (7): 669–684.

Grice, Herbert P. 1975. "Logic and Conversation." In *Speech and Semantics, Vol. 3, Speech Acts*, edited by Peter Cole and Jerry L. Morgan, 41–58. New York: Academic Press.

Hajnal, Zoltan L. 2001. "White Residents, Black Incumbents, and a Declining Racial Divide." *American Political Science Review* 95 (3): 603–618.

Halevy, Nir, Ori Weisel, and Gary Bornstein. 2012. "'In-Group Love' and 'Out-Group Hate' in Repeated Interaction Between Groups." *Journal of Behavioral Decision Making* 25 (2): 188–195.

Hamilton, Alexander, James Madison, and John Jay. 2014. *The Federalist Papers*. New York: Courier Corporation.

Harber, Kent D., Douglas Yeung, and Anthony Iacovelli. 2011. "Psychosocial Resources, Threat, and the Perception of Distance and Height: Support for the Resources and Perception Model." *Emotion* 11 (5): 1080–1090.

Hawley, George. 2011. "Political Threat and Immigration: Party Identification, Demographic Context, and Immigration Policy Preference." *Social Science Quarterly* 92 (2): 404–422.

Hopkins, Daniel J. 2010. "Politicized Places: Explaining Where and When Immigrants Provoke Local Opposition." *American Political Science Review* 104 (1): 40–60.

2014. "One Language, Two Meanings: Partisanship and Responses to Spanish." *Political Communication* 31 (3): 421–445.

Howe, Lauren C., and Jon A. Krosnick. 2017. "Attitude Strength." *Annual Review of Psychology* 68 (1): 327–351. https://doi.org/10.1146/annurev-psych-122414-033600.

Huddy, Leonie, and Stanley Feldman. 2009. "On Assessing the Political Effects of Racial Prejudice." *Annual Review of Political Science* 12: 423–447.

Husnu, Senel, and Richard John Crisp. 2011. "Enhancing the Imagined Contact Effect." *The Journal of Social Psychology* 151 (1): 113–116.

Iyengar, Shanto, Gaurav Sood, and Yphtach Lelkes. 2012. "Affect, Not Ideology A Social Identity Perspective on Polarization." *Public Opinion Quarterly* 76 (3): 405–431.

Jackman, Mary R. 1978. "General and Applied Tolerance: Does Education Increase Commitment to Racial Integration?" *American Journal of Political Science* 22 (2): 302–324.

——— 1996. "Individualism, Self-Interest, and White Racism." *Social Science Quarterly* 77 (4): 760–767.

Jackman, Mary R., and Marie Crane. 1986. "'Some of My Best Friends Are Black … ': Interracial Friendship and Whites' Racial Attitudes." *The Public Opinion Quarterly* 50 (4): 459–486.

Jardina, Ashley. 2019. *White Identity Politics*. New York: Cambridge University Press.

Jost, John T., Jaime L. Napier, Hulda Thorisdottir, Samuel D. Gosling, Tibor P. Palfai, and Brian Ostafin. 2007. "Are Needs to Manage Uncertainty and Threat Associated with Political Conservatism or Ideological Extremity?" *Personality and Social Psychology Bulletin* 33 (7): 989–1007.

Kam, Cindy D., and Donald R. Kinder. 2012. "Ethnocentrism as a Short-Term Force in the 2008 American Presidential Election." *American Journal of Political Science* 56 (2): 326–340.

Key, Valdimer Orlando. 1949. *Southern Politics in a State and Nation*. New York: A.A. Knopf.

Kinder, Donald R, and Nathan P. Kalmoe. 2017. *Neither Liberal Nor Conservative: Ideological Innocence in the American Public*. Chicago: University of Chicago Press.

Kinder, Donald R., and Cindy D. Kam. 2009. *Us against Them: Ethnocentric Foundations of American Opinion*. Chicago Studies in American Politics. Chicago: University of Chicago Press.

Kinder, Donald R., and David O. Sears. 1981. "Prejudice and Politics: Symbolic Racism versus Racial Threats to the Good Life." *Journal of Personality and Social Psychology* 40 (3): 414–431.

King, Desmond S., and Rogers M. Smith. 2011. *Still a House Divided: Race and Politics in Obama's America*. Princeton: Princeton University Press.

——— 2014. "'Without Regard to Race': Critical Ideational Development in Modern American Politics." *The Journal of Politics* 76 (04): 958–971.

Kirwan institute for the study of race and ethnicity. 2010. "Talking about Race: Toward a Transformative Agenda." The Ohio State University. www.intergroupresources.com/rc/TAR%20notebook.pdf.

Klar, Samara. 2013. "The Influence of Competing Identity Primes on Political Preferences." *The Journal of Politics* 75 (4): 1108–1124.

Knobloch-Westerwick, Silvia, and Jingbo Meng. 2009. "Looking the Other Way: Selective Exposure to Attitude-Consistent and Counterattitudinal Political Information." *Communication Research* 36 (3): 426–448.

Koudenburg, Namkje, Tom Postmes, and Ernestine H. Gordijn. 2013. "Conversational Flow Promotes Solidarity." *PLOS ONE* 8 (11): e78363.

Krogstad, Jens Manuel, and Mark Hugo Lopez. 2016. "Hillary Clinton Wins Latino Vote, but Falls below 2012 Support for Obama." *Pew Research Center*, November 9, 2016. www.pewresearch.org/fact-tank/2016/11/09/hillary-clinton-wins-latino-vote-but-falls-below-2012-support-for-obama/.

Lakens, Daniël. 2017. "Equivalence Tests: A Practical Primer for t Tests, Correlations, and Meta-Analyses." *Social Psychological and Personality Science* 8 (4): 355–362.

Leighley, Jan E., and Arnold Vedlitz. 1999. "Race, Ethnicity, and Political Participation: Competing Models and Contrasting Explanations." *Journal of Politics* 61 (4): 1092–1114.

Lelkes, Yphtach, and Sean J. Westwood. 2017. "The Limits of Partisan Prejudice." *The Journal of Politics* 79 (2): 485–501.

Leonardelli, Geoffrey J., Cynthia L. Pickett, and Marilynn B. Brewer. 2010. "Optimal Distinctiveness Theory: A Framework for Social Identity, Social Cognition, and Intergroup Relations." In *Advances in Experimental Social Psychology, Vol. 43*, edited by Mark P. Zanna and James M. Olson, 63–113. New York: Elsevier.

Lick, David J., and Kerri L. Johnson. 2015. "The Interpersonal Consequences of Processing Ease: Fluency as a Metacognitive Foundation for Prejudice." *Current Directions in Psychological Science* 24 (2): 143–148.

Loewenstein, G. F., E. U. Weber, C. K. Hsee, and N. Welch. 2001. "Risk as Feelings." *Psychological Bulletin* 127 (2): 267–286.

Lukes, Steven. 1974. *Power: A Radical View*. London: Macmillan.

MacInnis, Cara C., and Elizabeth Page-Gould. 2015. "How Can Intergroup Interaction Be Bad If Intergroup Contact Is Good? Exploring and Reconciling an Apparent Paradox in the Science of Intergroup Relations." *Perspectives on Psychological Science* 10 (3): 307–327.

Macrae, C. Neil, and Susanne Quadflieg. 2010. "Perceiving People." In *Handbook of Social Psychology*, edited by Susan T. Fiske, Daniel T. Gilbert, and Gardner Lindzey, 5th ed., 428–463. Hoboken, NJ: John Wiley & Sons.

Major, Brenda, Alison Blodorn, and Gregory Major Blascovich. 2018. "The Threat of Increasing Diversity: Why Many White Americans Support Trump in the 2016 Presidential Election." *Group Processes & Intergroup Relations* 21 (6): 931–940.

Mansbridge, Jane J., James Bohman, Simone Chambers, Thomas Christiano, Archon Fung, John Parkinson, Dennis F. Thompson, and Mark E. Warren. 2012. "A Systemic Approach to Deliberative Democracy." In *Deliberative*

Systems, edited by John Parkinson and Jane Mansbridge, 1–26. Cambridge: Cambridge University Press.

Mansbridge, Jane J., James Bohman, Simone Chambers, David Estlund, Andreas Føllesdal, Archon Fung, Cristina Lafont, Bernard Manin, et al. 2010. "The Place of Self-Interest and the Role of Power in Deliberative Democracy." *Journal of Political Philosophy* 18 (1): 64–100.

Martin, Judith N., and Michael L. Hecht. 1994. "Conversational Improvement Strategies for Interethnic Communication: African American and European American Perspectives." *Communication Monographs* 61 (3): 236–255.

Mason, Lilliana. 2018. *Uncivil Agreement: How Politics Became Our Identity.* Chicago: University of Chicago Press.

McDermott, Rose. 2002. "Experimental Methodology in Political Science." *Political Analysis* 10 (4): 325–342.

Meegan, Daniel V. 2010. "Zero-Sum Bias: Perceived Competition Despite Unlimited Resources." *Frontiers in Psychology* 1:191.

Mendelberg, Tali. 2001. *The Race Card: Campaign Strategy, Implicit Messages, and the Norm of Equality.* Princeton: Princeton University Press.

Mendes, Wendy Berry, Jim Blascovich, Sarah B. Hunter, Brian Lickel, and John T. Jost. 2007. "Threatened by the Unexpected: Physiological Responses during Social Interactions with Expectancy-Violating Partners." *Journal of Personality and Social Psychology* 92 (4): 698–716.

Moskos, Charles, and John Sibley Butler. 1996. *All That We Can Be: Black Leadership And Racial Integration The Army Way.* New York: Basic Books.

Motyl, Matt, Ravi Iyer, Shigehiro Oishi, Sophie Trawalter, and Brian A. Nosek. 2014. "How Ideological Migration Geographically Segregates Groups." *Journal of Experimental Social Psychology* 51: 1–14.

Mullinix, Kevin J., Thomas J. Leeper, James N. Druckman, and Jeremy Freese. 2015. "The Generalizability of Survey Experiments." *Journal of Experimental Political Science* 2 (2): 109–138.

Mutz, Diana C. 2018. "Status Threat, Not Economic Hardship, Explains the 2016 Presidential Vote." *Proceedings of the National Academy of Sciences* 115 (19): e4330-e4339.

Newman, Benjamin J. 2014. "My Poor Friend: Financial Distress in One's Social Network, the Perceived Power of the Rich, and Support for Redistribution." *The Journal of Politics* 76 (1): 126–138.

Nisbett, Richard E., and Dov Cohen. 1996. *Culture Of Honor: The Psychology Of Violence In The South.* New Directions in Social Psychology: Self, Cognition & Collectives. New York: Routledge.

Norton, Michael I., and Samuel R. Sommers. 2011. "Whites See Racism as a Zero-Sum Game That They Are Now Losing." *Perspectives on Psychological Science* 6 (3): 215–218.

Nummenmaa, Lauri, and Andrew J. Calder. 2009. "Neural Mechanisms of Social Attention." *Trends in Cognitive Sciences* 13 (3): 135–143.

Nygaard, Lynne C., and Erin R. Lunders. 2002. "Resolution of Lexical Ambiguity by Emotional Tone of Voice." *Memory & Cognition* 30 (4): 583–593.

Nygaard, Lynne C., and Jennifer S. Queen. 2008. "Communicating Emotion: Linking Affective Prosody and Word Meaning." *Journal of Experimental Psychology: Human Perception and Performance* 34 (4): 1017–1030.

Oeberst, Aileen, and Johannes Moskaliuk. 2016. "Classic Conversational Norms in Modern Computer-Mediated Collaboration." *Journal of Educational Technology & Society* 19 (1): 187–198.

Oliver, J. Eric. 2010. *The Paradoxes of Integration: Race, Neighborhood, and Civic Life in Multiethnic America.* Chicago: University of Chicago Press.

Oliver, J. Eric, and Tali Mendelberg. 2000. "Reconsidering the Environmental Determinants of White Racial Attitudes." *American Journal of Political Science* 44 (3): 574–589.

Open Science Collaboration. 2015. "Estimating the Reproducibility of Psychological Science." *Science* 349 (6251): aac4716–aac4716.

Oppenheimer, Daniel M. 2008. "The Secret Life of Fluency." *Trends in Cognitive Sciences* 12 (6): 237–241.

Paluck, Elizabeth Levy, Seth A. Green, and Donald P. Green. 2019. "The Contact Hypothesis Re-Evaluated." *Behavioural Public Policy* 3 (2): 129–158.

Paolini, Stefania, Jake Harwood, and Mark Rubin. 2010. "Negative Intergroup Contact Makes Group Memberships Salient: Explaining Why Intergroup Conflict Endures." *Personality and Social Psychology Bulletin* 36 (12): 1723–1738.

Paolini, Stefania, Jake Harwood, Mark Rubin, Shenel Husnu, Nicholas Joyce, and Miles Hewstone. 2014. "Positive and Extensive Intergroup Contact in the Past Buffers against the Disproportionate Impact of Negative Contact in the Present." *European Journal of Social Psychology* 44 (6): 548–562.

Park, Bernadette, Christopher Wolsko, and Charles M. Judd. 2001. "Measurement of Subtyping in Stereotype Change." *Journal of Experimental Social Psychology* 37 (4): 325–332.

Patchen, Martin. 1982. *Black-White Contact in Schools: Its Social and Academic Effects.* West Lafayette: Purdue University Press.

Pearson, Adam R., and John F. Dovidio. 2014. "Intergroup Fluency: How Processing Experiences Shape Intergroup Cognition and Communication." In *Social Cognition and Communication*, edited by Joseph P. Forgas, Orsoyla Vincze, and Janos Laszlo, 101–120. The Sydney Symposium of Social Psychology. New York: Psychology Press.

Pearson, Adam R., Tessa V. West, John F. Dovidio, Stacie Renfro Powers, Ross Buck, and Robert Henning. 2008. "The Fragility of Intergroup Relations: Divergent Effects of Delayed Audiovisual Feedback in Intergroup and Intragroup Interaction." *Psychological Science* 19 (12): 1272–1279.

Pearson-Merkowitz, Shanna, Alexandra Filindra, and Joshua J. Dyck. 2016. "When Partisans and Minorities Interact: Interpersonal Contact, Partisanship, and Public Opinion Preferences on Immigration Policy." *Social Science Quarterly* 97: 311–324.

Perrett, D. I., P. A. J. Smith, D. D. Potter, A. J. Mistlin, A. S. Head, A. D. Milner, and M. A. Jeeves. 1985. "Visual Cells in the Temporal Cortex Sensitive to Face View and Gaze Direction." *Proceedings of the Royal Society of London. Series B, Biological Sciences* 223 (1232): 293–317.

Pesarin, Fortunato, and Luigi Salmaso. 2010. *Permutation Tests for Complex Data: Theory, Applications and Software*. 1st ed. Hoboken, NJ: John Wiley & Sons.

Petronio, Sandra, Naomi Ellemers, Howard Giles, and Cynthia Gallois. 1998. "(Mis) Communicating across Boundaries: Interpersonal and Intergroup Considerations." *Communication Research* 25 (6): 571–595.

Pettigrew, Thomas F. 1969. "Rejoinder." *Journal of Social Issues* 25 (4): 201–205.

1998. "Intergroup Contact Theory." *Annual Review of Psychology* 49 (1): 65–85.

2008. "Reflections on Core Themes in Intergroup Research." In *Improving Intergroup Relations*, edited by Ulrich Wagner, Linda R. Tropp, Gillian Finchilescu, and Colin Tredoux, 281–303. Oxford: Blackwell Publishing Ltd.

Pettigrew, Thomas F., and Linda R. Tropp. 2006. "A Meta-Analytic Test of Intergroup Contact Theory." *Journal of Personality and Social Psychology* 90 (5): 751–783.

2011. *When Groups Meet: The Dynamics of Intergroup Contact*. Essays in Social Psychology. New York: Psychology Press.

Quillian, Lincoln. 1995. "Prejudice as a Response to Perceived Group Threat: Population Composition and Anti-Immigrant and Racial Prejudice in Europe." *American Sociological Review* 60 (4): 586–611.

Rabinowitz, Joshua L., David O. Sears, Jim Sidanius, and Jon A. Krosnick. 2009. "Why Do White Americans Oppose Race-Targeted Policies? Clarifying the Impact of Symbolic Racism." *Political Psychology* 30 (5): 805–828.

Reimer, Nils Karl, Julia C. Becker, Angelika Benz, Oliver Christ, Kristof Dhont, Ulrich Klocke, Sybille Neji, Magdalena Rychlowska, Katharina Schmid, and Miles Hewstone. 2017. "Intergroup Contact and Social Change: Implications of Negative and Positive Contact for Collective Action in Advantaged and Disadvantaged Groups." *Personality and Social Psychology Bulletin* 43 (1): 121–136.

Reisenzein, Rainer. 1986. "A Structural Equation Analysis of Weiner's Attribution—Affect Model of Helping Behavior." *Journal of Personality and Social Psychology* 50 (6): 1123–1133.

Reny, Tyler T., Ali A. Valenzuela, and Loren Collingwood. 2020. "'No, You're Playing the Race Card': Testing the Effects of Anti-Black, Anti-Latino, and Anti-Immigrant Appeals in the Post-Obama Era." *Political Psychology* 42 (2): 283–302.

Richards, Zoeë, and Miles Hewstone. 2001. "Subtyping and Subgrouping: Processes for the Prevention and Promotion of Stereotype Change." *Personality and Social Psychology Review* 5 (1): 52–73.

Richeson, Jennifer A., Abigail A. Baird, Heather L. Gordon, Todd F. Heatherton, Carrie L. Wyland, Sophie Trawalter, and J. Nicole Shelton. 2003. "An FMRI Investigation of the Impact of Interracial Contact on Executive Function." *Nature Neuroscience* 6 (12): 1323–1328.

Riek, Blake M., Eric W. Mania, and Samuel L. Gaertner. 2006. "Intergroup Threat and Outgroup Attitudes: A Meta-Analytic Review." *Personality and Social Psychology Review* 10 (4): 336–353.

Riordan, Cornelius. 1978. "Equal-Status Interracial Contact: A Review and Revision of the Concept." *International Journal of Intercultural Relations* 2 (2): 161–185.

Riordan, Cornelius, and Josephine Ruggiero. 1980. "Producing Equal-Status Interracial Interaction: A Replication." *Social Psychology Quarterly* 43 (1): 131–136.

Robinson, Jerry W., and James D. Preston. 1976. "Equal-Status Contact and Modification of Racial Prejudice: A Reexamination of the Contact Hypothesis." *Social Forces* 54 (4): 911–924.

Rothschild, Jacob E., Adam J. Howat, Richard M. Shafranek, and Ethan C. Busby. 2019. "Pigeonholing Partisans: Stereotypes of Party Supporters and Partisan Polarization." *Political Behavior* 41 (2): 423–443.

Rubin, Mark, Stefania Paolini, and Richard J. Crisp. 2010. "A Processing Fluency Explanation of Bias against Migrants." *Journal of Experimental Social Psychology* 46 (1): 21–28.

Rugh, Jacob S., and Douglas S. Massey. 2014. "Segregation in Post-Civil Rights America: Stalled Integration or End of the Segregated Century?" *Du Bois Review: Social Science Research on Race* 11 (2): 205–232.

Sagiv, Lilach, and Shalom H. Schwartz. 1995. "Value Priorities and Readiness for Out-Group Social Contact." *Journal of Personality and Social Psychology* 69 (3): 437–448.

Saguy, Tamar, and Lily Chernyak-Hai. 2012. "Intergroup Contact Can Undermine Disadvantaged Group Members' Attributions to Discrimination." *Journal of Experimental Social Psychology* 48 (3): 714–720.

Saguy, Tamar, Nicole Tausch, John F. Dovidio, and Felicia Pratto. 2009. "The Irony of Harmony: Intergroup Contact Can Produce False Expectations for Equality." *Psychological Science* 20 (1): 114–121.

Sanders, Lynn M. 1997. "Against Deliberation." *Political Theory* 25 (3): 347–376.

Sands, Melissa L. 2017. "Exposure to Inequality Affects Support for Redistribution." *Proceedings of the National Academy of Sciences* 114 (4): 663–668.

Schmidt, Greg, and Bernard Weiner. 1988. "An Attribution-Affect-Action Theory of Behavior: Replications of Judgments of Help-Giving." *Personality and Social Psychology Bulletin* 14 (3): 610–621.

Schröder, Tobias, and Paul Thagard. 2013. "The Affective Meanings of Automatic Social Behaviors: Three Mechanisms That Explain Priming." *Psychological Review* 120 (1): 255–280.

Schwartz, Shalom H. 2003. "A Proposal for Measuring Value Orientations across Nations." Questionnaire Package of the European Social Survey, 259–290.

Schwartz, Shalom H., Gian Vittorio Caprara, Michele Vecchione, Paul Bain, Gabriel Bianchi, Maria Giovanna Caprara, Jan Cieciuch, et al. 2014. "Basic Personal Values Underlie and Give Coherence to Political Values: A Cross National Study in 15 Countries." *Political Behavior* 36 (4): 899–930.

Schwarz, Norbert. 2004. "Meta-Cognitive Experiences in Consumer Judgment and Decision Making." *Journal of Consumer Psychology* 14 (4): 332–348.

Schwarz, Norbert, and Gerald L. Clore. 2003. "Mood as Information: 20 Years Later." *Psychological Inquiry* 14 (3/4): 296–303.

Sears, David O. 1986. "College Sophomores in the Laboratory: Influences of a Narrow Data Base on Social Psychology's View of Human Nature." *Journal of Personality and Social Psychology* 51 (3): 515–530.

Senju, Atsushi, and Mark H. Johnson. 2009. "The Eye Contact Effect: Mechanisms and Development." *Trends in Cognitive Sciences* 13 (3): 127–134.

Shepherd, Stephen V. 2010. "Following Gaze: Gaze-Following Behavior as a Window into Social Cognition." *Frontiers in Integrative Neuroscience* 4, Article 5.

Shook, Natalie J., and Russell H. Fazio. 2008. "Interracial Roommate Relationships An Experimental Field Test of the Contact Hypothesis." *Psychological Science* 19 (7): 717–723.

Sigelman, Lee, Timothy Bledsoe, Susan Welch, and Michael W. Combs. 1996. "Making Contact? Black-White Social Interaction in an Urban Setting." *American Journal of Sociology* 101 (5): 1306–1332.

Sønderskov, Kim Mannemar, and Jens Peter Frølund Thomsen. 2015. "Contextualizing Intergroup Contact Do Political Party Cues Enhance Contact Effects?" *Social Psychology Quarterly* 78 (1): 49–76.

Soss, Joe, Richard C. Fording, and Sanford Schram. 2011. *Disciplining the Poor: Neoliberal Paternalism and the Persistent Power of Race*. Chicago Studies in American Politics. Chicago: University of Chicago Press.

Steakin, Will, and Rachel Scott. 2019. "Vice President Pence Rolls out 'Latinos for Trump,' Slams Democrats Ahead of Debate." *ABC News*, June 25, 2019. https://abcnews.go.com/Politics/trump-rolling-coalition-aimed-courting-hispanic-voters/story?id=63841872.

Stringer, Maurice, P. Irwing, M. Giles, C. McClenahan, R. Wilson, and J. A. Hunter. 2009. "Intergroup Contact, Friendship Quality and Political Attitudes in Integrated and Segregated Schools in Northern Ireland." *British Journal of Educational Psychology* 79 (2): 239–257.

Sullivan, John L., James Piereson, and George E. Marcus. 1982. *Political Tolerance and American Democracy*. Chicago: University of Chicago Press.

Swart, Hermann, Miles Hewstone, Oliver Christ, and Alberto Voci. 2011. "Affective Mediators of Intergroup Contact: A Three-Wave Longitudinal Study in South Africa." *Journal of Personality and Social Psychology* 101 (6): 1221–1238.

Tajfel, Henri. 1978. *Differentiation between Social Groups: Studies in the Social Psychology of Intergroup Relations*. London: Academic Press.

1982. "Social Psychology of Intergroup Relations." *Annual Review of Psychology* 33 (1): 1–39.

Taylor, Charles. 1994. "The Politics of Recognition." In *Multiculturalism*, edited by Amy Guttmann, 99–103. Princeton: Princeton University Press.

Thompson, Dennis F. 2008. "Deliberative Democratic Theory and Empirical Political Science." *Annual Review of Political Science* 11 (1): 497–520.

Toosi, Negin R., Laura G. Babbitt, Nalini Ambady, and Samuel R. Sommers. 2012. "Dyadic Interracial Interactions: A Meta-Analysis." *Psychological Bulletin* 138 (1): 1–27.

Trawalter, Sophie, and Jennifer A. Richeson. 2008. "Let's Talk about Race, Baby! When Whites' and Blacks' Interracial Contact Experiences Diverge." *Journal of Experimental Social Psychology* 44 (4): 1214–1217.

Tropp, Linda R., Dina G. Okamoto, Helen B. Marrow, and Michael Jones-Correa. 2018. "How Contact Experiences Shape Welcoming: Perspectives from U.S.-Born and Immigrant Groups." *Social Psychology Quarterly* 81 (1): 23–47.

Tuch, Steven A., and Michael Hughes. 2011. "Whites' Racial Policy Attitudes in the Twenty-First Century: The Continuing Significance of Racial Resentment." *The ANNALS of the American Academy of Political and Social Science* 634 (1): 134–152.

Turner, Rhiannon N., Miles Hewstone, Alberto Voci, Stefania Paolini, and Oliver Christ. 2007. "Reducing Prejudice via Direct and Extended Cross-Group Friendship." *European Review of Social Psychology* 18 (1): 212–255.

Tversky, Amos, and Daniel Kahneman. 1974. "Judgment under Uncertainty: Heuristics and Biases." *Science* 185 (4157): 1124–1131.

Valentino, Nicholas A., Fabian G. Neuner, and L. Matthew Vandenbroek. 2018. "The Changing Norms of Racial Political Rhetoric and the End of Racial Priming." *The Journal of Politics* 80 (3): 757–771.

Vermue, Marieke, Charles R. Seger, and Alan G. Sanfey. 2018. "Group-Based Biases Influence Learning about Individual Trustworthiness." *Journal of Experimental Social Psychology* 77 (July): 36–49.

Voci, Alberto, and Miles Hewstone. 2003. "Intergroup Contact and Prejudice toward Immigrants in Italy: The Mediational Role of Anxiety and the Moderational Role of Group Salience." *Group Processes & Intergroup Relations* 6 (1): 37–54.

Walsh, Katherine Cramer. 2007. *Talking about Race: Community Dialogues and the Politics of Difference*. Chicago: University of Chicago Press.

Weir, Margaret. 1992. "Ideas and the Politics of Bounded Innovation." In *Structuring Politics: Historical Institutionalism in Comparative Analysis*, edited by Sven Steinmo, Kathleen Ann Thelen, and

Frank Longstreth, 188–216. Cambridge Studies in Comparative Politics. New York: Cambridge University Press.

White, Fiona A., Lauren J. Harvey, and Hisham M. Abu-Rayya. 2015. "Improving Intergroup Relations in the Internet Age: A Critical Review." *Review of General Psychology* 19 (2): 129–139.

Wilkins, Clara L., and Cheryl R. Kaiser. 2014. "Racial Progress as Threat to the Status Hierarchy: Implications for Perceptions of Anti-White Bias." *Psychological Science* 25 (2): 439–446.

Wilkins, Clara L., Joseph D. Wellman, Laura G. Babbitt, Negin R. Toosi, and Katherine D. Schad. 2015. "You Can Win but I Can't Lose: Bias against High-Status Groups Increases Their Zero-Sum Beliefs about Discrimination." *Journal of Experimental Social Psychology* 57 (March): 1–14.

Wilner, Daniel M., Rosabelle Price Walkley, and Stuart W. Cook. 1955. *Human Relations in Interracial Housing: A Study of the Contact Hypothesis.* 1st ed. Minneapolis: University of Minnesota Press.

Xiao, Y. Jenny, and Jay J. Van Bavel. 2012. "See Your Friends Close and Your Enemies Closer: Social Identity and Identity Threat Shape the Representation of Physical Distance." *Personality and Social Psychology Bulletin* 38 (7): 959–972.

Zaller, John, and Stanley Feldman. 1992. "A Simple Theory of the Survey Response: Answering Questions versus Revealing Preferences." *American Journal of Political Science* 36 (3): 579–616.

Acknowledgments

I would like to thank many colleagues for their invaluable advice and support in producing this Element. Jamie Druckman provided countless hours of advice and guidance in the development of this Element. Julie Lee Merseth and Reuel Rogers also gave a great deal of critical advice and support on this research. A portion of this design was presented at the 2018 annual meeting of the Midwest Political Science Association – I am grateful for the suggestions of Cara Wong and other participants in that panel. Other parts of this Element were presented at the LDS Scholars Workshop at Brigham Young University, where the participants gave great comments and suggestions that dramatically improved this Element. The Druckman research lab at Northwestern University also provided countless pages and hours of detailed advice, and I am indebted to them for so much of this project. I also appreciate the help of the pollsters and lab administrators who helped execute these experiments. In addition, I am grateful for those who provided feedback on the oral version of various parts of this Element, including the American Politics Workshop at Northwestern University, Chloe Thurston, Rana Khoury, Matthew Lacombe, Sean Diament, Adam Howat, Andrew Thompson, Sasha Klyachkina, Adam Dynes, Chris Karpowitz, and Josh Gubler. Countless friends and family members discussed and piloted these studies with no expectation of payment or recognition. Above all else, I am grateful to my wife, Andrea, for countless hours of research, practical, and emotional support and my daughter, Ruth, for just as many hours of inspiration and joy.

This research could not have been conducted without generous support from various grants from the Department of Political Science at Northwestern University, The Graduate School at Northwestern, the Department of Political Science at Clemson University, and the Marguerite Ross Barnett Fund of the American Political Science Association.

Cambridge Elements ≡

Experimental Political Science

James N. Druckman
Northwestern University
James N. Druckman is the Payson S. Wild Professor of Political Science and Faculty Fellow at the Institute for Policy Research at Northwestern University. More information about him can be found at: https://faculty.wcas.northwestern.edu/~jnd260/

About the Series
There currently are few outlets for extended works on experimental methodology in political science. The *Experimental Political Science* Cambridge Elements series features research on experimental approaches to a given substantive topic, and experimental methods by prominent and upcoming experts in the field.

Cambridge Elements ☰

Experimental Political Science

Elements in the Series

Printed in the United States
by Baker & Taylor Publisher Services